Living Spring

Francisco Candido Xavier

Living Spring

Dictated by the spirit
Emmanuel

Copyright © 2012 by
BRAZILIAN SPIRITIST FEDERATION
Av. L 2 Norte – Q. 603 – Conjunto F (SGAN)
70830-030 – Brasilia (DF) – Brazil

All rights reserved. No part of this book may be reproduced by any mechanical, photographic, or electronic process, or in the form of a phonographic recording; nor may it be stored in a retrieval system, transmitted, or otherwise be copied for public or private use without prior written permission of the publisher.

ISBN: 978-1-936547-92-0

Original title in Portuguese:
FONTE VIVA
Brazil, 1956

Translated by: Darrel Kimble and Marcia Saiz

Cover design by: Evelyn Yuri Furuta
Layout: Luciano Carneiro Holanda

Edition of
EDICEI OF AMERICA
8425 Biscayne Boulevard. Suite 104.
Miami, FL 33138
(305) 758-7444
www.ediceiofamerica.com
info@ediceiofamerica.com

First Edition – 9/2013

Authorized edition by Brazilian Spiritist Federation

INTERNATIONAL DATA FOR CATALOGING IN PUBLICATION (ICP)

E54s

Emmanuel (Spirit)

  Living spring / dictated by the spirit Emmanuel ; [received by] Francisco Cândido Xavier ; translated by Darrel W. Kimble and Marcia Saiz. – Miami, FL, USA : Edicei of America, 2013.
  380 p. ; 21 cm

  Original title: Fonte Viva
  ISBN 978-1-936547-92-0

  1. Spiritualism. 2. Bible and spiritualism. I. Xavier, Francisco Cândido, 1910-2002. II. Title.

CDD 133.93
CDU 133.7

Contents

With Jesus and for Jesus 11
1 - In Light of the Lesson 15
2 - The Way to Do It 17
3 - On the Great Journey 19
4 - Each One 21
5 - Can You Go? 23
6 - Accept the Correction 25
7 - By Their Fruit 27
8 - Attentive Workers 29
9 - Let Us Be Content 31
10 - Yes, Indeed 33
11 - Let Us Glorify 35
12 - Impediments 37
13 - Let Us Set Out 39
14 - An Opportune Question 41
15 - Fraternity 43
16 - Be Not Troubled 45
17 - Christ and Us 47
18 - Not Only 49
19 - Feeding 51
20 - Difference 53
21 - Greatness 55

22 - The Reward	57
23 - Before the Sublime	59
24 - By Their Works	61
25 - Concerning Christ's Gifts	63
26 - A Worker without Faith	65
27 - Destruction and Misery	67
28 - Something	69
29 - Let Us Serve	71
30 - Educate	73
31 - Farmers	75
32 - The Good Part	77
33 - Raising and Helping	79
34 - Let us be Alert	81
35 - Let Us Spread the Good	83
36 - Clarifying Affirmation	85
37 - In the Regenerative Work	87
38 - If We only Knew	89
39 - Inoperative Faith	91
40 - Concerning the Objective	93
41 - On the Difficult Road	95
42 - For a Short Time	97
43 - Language	99
44 - Let Us Have Faith	101
45 - Only in this Way	103
46 - On the Cross	105
47 - Self-Liberation	107
48 - In the Lord's Presence	109
49 - Fraternal Union	111
50 - Let Us Go Forward	113
51 - Open Graves	115
52 - Serving and Progressing	117
53 - On Preaching	119

54 - Let Us Seek Eagerly 121
55 - Elucidations 123
56 - Be Born again Now 125
57 - Apostles 127
58 - Disciples 129
59 - Words of Eternal Life 131
60 - Alms 133
61 - Never Give Up 135
62 - Slowly but Surely 137
63 - Differences 139
64 - Sowers 141
65 - Be Not Deceived 143
66 - Up and Rise 145
67 - Inner Renewal 147
68 - Sowing and Construction 149
69 - Firmness and Perseverance 151
70 - Loneliness 153
71 - Take the Opportunity 155
72 - Incomprehension 157
73 - Fraternal Encouragement 159
74 - When there is Light 161
75 - Management 163
76 - Spiritual Yeast 165
77 - Our Father 167
78 - Divine Grafting 169
79 - Let Us Follow Peace 171
80 - Fattened Hearts 173
81 - The Living Lamp 175
82 - The One Who Serves Goes Forward 177
83 - Let Us Go Further 179
84 - Instruments 181
85 - Obstacles 183

86 - Are You Sick? 185
87 - Did You Receive the Light? 189
88 - Coming to One's Senses 191
89 - On Our Journey 193
90 - Courageously 195
91 - Matters of the Heart 197
92 - Signs from Heaven 199
93 - The Inner Altar 201
94 - The Helmet of Hope 203
95 - See and Go Forward 205
96 - Go beyond what Others Do 207
97 - The Message of the Cross 209
98 - The Breastplate of Charity 211
99 - Persevere and Press On 213
100 - Absentees 215
101 - The Veil of "Self" 217
102 - Let Us Be Joyful Always 219
103 - Waiting and Receiving 221
104 - In the Presence of the Crowd 223
105 - You Are the Light 225
106 - Let Us Serve the Good 227
107 - Let Us Renew Ourselves Each Day 229
108 - A Little Yeast 231
109 - Christ's Example 233
110 - Let Us Watch and Pray 235
111 - Let Us Strengthen Ourselves 237
112 - What Am I To Do? 239
113 - Let Us Seek the Best 241
114 - Put Away Your Sword 243
115 - Let Us Remain Loyal 245
116 - Go and Teach 247
117 - We Have what We Give 249

118 - In Our Endeavors 251
119 - Listen Now 253
120 - Thus It Will Be 255
121 - Let Us Seek the Light 257
122 - Let Us Understand One Another 259
123 - Living in Peace 261
124 - Do Not Become Weary 263
125 - Richly 265
126 - Let Us Help Always 267
127 - Royal Humanity 269
128 - Do Not Discard Your Confidence 271
129 - Be Patient 273
130 - In the Inner Sphere 275
131 - In the Social Arena 277
132 - Being Afraid 279
133 - What Do You Have? 281
134 - Let Us Seek Balance 283
135 - Forgive Always 285
136 - Let Us Live Peaceably 287
137 - Let Us Attend To the Good 289
138 - The Right Remedy 291
139 - Concerning the Work of Salvation 293
140 - Behind Jesus 295
141 - Renew Yourself Always 297
142 - Do Not Steal 299
143 - Wake Up and Help 301
144 - Let Us Assist the Mental Life 303
145 - Beware of the Dogs 305
146 - Let Us Work Together 307
147 - Seek Refuge in Peace 311
148 - The Father's Heir 315
149 - The Adoration of Prayer 317

150 - The Prayer of a Righteous Person 319
151 - Slander.. 321
152 - Come 323
153 - Let Us Heed 325
154 - No One Lives solely for Himself 327
155 - Let Us Learn To Give Thanks................................ 329
156 - Relatives.. 331
157 - Children 333
158 - Without Love.. 335
159 - With Love... 337
160 - In the Everyday Struggle 339
161 - In the Common Effort... 341
162 - Within the Struggle... 343
163 - Let Us Learn with Jesus 345
164 - In God's Presence 347
165 - Do Not Doubt... 349
166 - Let Us Follow Him 351
167 - Let Us Watch Ourselves 353
168 - Between the Cradle and the Grave 355
169 - Let Us Seek Eternity.. 357
170 - Labeling... 359
171 - Bearing Witness 361
172 - Before Christ, the Liberator 363
173 - Before the Light of the Truth................................ 365
174 - Out-Stretched Hands 367
175 - Change 369
176 - Need for the Good.. 371
177 - Wealth for Heaven 373
178 - Reverence and Compassion................................... 375
179 - Let Us Watch Our Hands 377
180 - Christmas 379

With Jesus and for Jesus

In the introduction of *The Spirits' Book*[1], Allan Kardec makes this meaningful statement:

"Communications between the spirit world and the corporeal world belong to nature itself and there is nothing supernatural about them. That is why we have found traces of such communications among all cultures and throughout history. Nowadays, they are commonplace and obvious to the whole world."

In sect. VIII of the Conclusion of the same book, the Codifier confidently states:

"Jesus came to show humankind the road of true goodness. Since God sent him to remind humans of God's forgotten law, why would God not send the Spirits to remind them more precisely, now that they have forgotten it for the sake of pride and cupidity?"[2]

We know that, among other important issues, that great book containing the fundamentals of Spiritism deals with the laws of worship, labor, society, progress, equality, liberty, justice, love, charity, and moral perfection, as well as hopes and consolations.

---
[1] *The Spirits' Book,* Prolegomena. (International Spiritist Council, 3rd ed.)
[2] ibid

We make this reference to remind our readers that spirit phenomena have always been present in the world and in every evolutionary moment of humankind and that, from the beginning of the ministry to which he devoted himself, Allan Kardec stamped his work with the religious visage from which it could not absent itself, and he also emphasized the fact that Spiritism is strong because it is based on the same principles as religion: God, the soul and future rewards and punishments.

We fully accept the scientific and philosophical bases upon which the Spiritist Doctrine rests, bases that encourage us to acquire a "rational faith capable of looking reason straight in the face." Upon such bases, we have always seen Spiritism as representing restored Christianity, perfecting souls and renewing life on earth so that the Infinite Good may be victorious under the aegis of Christ, our Divine Master and Lord.

The apostle of the Spiritist Codification was fully aware of the lofty mandate regarding the principles he was compiling, and that is why that, from the very start, he concerned himself with the moral aspects in which the New Revelation was clothed, having stressed that Spiritism aims at making people better human beings, and as a consequence, making them happier by inspiring them to practice the purest evangelical morals.

We know that the crucible does not refine one's character and that philosophical argument has nothing to do with charity and justice. Therefore, with all our respect for philosophy, which asks questions, and for science, which provides answers, we will always recognize in Spiritism the active and renewed Gospel of the Lord for spreading, with Jesus, the Cosmic Religion of Universal Love and Divine Wisdom on earth.

There are millions of discarnate spirits of all levels of intelligence all over the world, and they are as much in need of the benefits of education as the incarnate ones are.

Thus, we cannot abide by those who make of our Redemptive Doctrine a mere tribunal for argumentation or a mere hunt for demonstrations of survival after death, a place for literary jousting, lengthy discussions and anecdotes without any spiritual consequences for their own path.

Let us study the lessons of the Divine Master and learn to practice them each and every day.

Death will bring us all together so that we may understand the true life ... And knowing that justice will define us according to our deeds, let us embrace Kardec's Codification and go forward with Jesus and for Jesus.

EMMANUEL
February 11, 1956,
City of Pedro Leopoldo, Brazil.

~ 1 ~

In Light of the Lesson

> *Consider well what I am telling you, for the Lord will give you understanding in everything.* – Paul (2 Tim. 2:7)

In light of an exposition of the truth, remember to ponder the lesson you have received.

Those who glance up at the sky without contemplating it will never really see the stars; those who listen to a symphony without opening up the acoustics of their soul will never perceive its divine notes.

Listening to the inspired words of ardent preachers will do you no good whatsoever if you do not open up your heart so that your sentiments may be immersed in their blessed light.

Countless followers of the Gospel complain about their inability to retain its teachings, claiming to be unfit in light of its new revelations. This is because they do not spend enough time meditating on its lessons, whereas they spend too much time on distractions and frivolity.

When a room is too dark, it is up to us to open the windows to let the sun shine in.

If we will dedicate a little effort to the blessing of the lesson, the lesson will answer us with its blessings.

The Apostle to the Gentiles is very clear when he says:

"Consider what I am telling you, for the Lord will give you understanding in everything."

To consider means to examine, hear, reflect, and evaluate.

Therefore, we can be sure that, in paying attention to the principles of the Code of Eternal Life, the Lord will reward our goodwill by giving us understanding in everything.

~ 2 ~

The Way to Do It

Let the same sentiment there be in you as was in Christ Jesus. – Paul. (Phil. 2:5)

Everyone does something in life, but there are very few who do not have to return to the flesh to undo what they have done.

Even lazy people who have spent their lives in uselessness and idleness have to return to the struggle in order to clear away the web of inertia that they have woven around themselves.

Only those inspired by Jesus' standard for doing good can conduct their lives in such a way that they will not have to make reparations or corrections later on.

Doing something in Christ means always doing the best for everybody:

Without expecting any kind of payment;
Without demanding anything;
Without putting on a show;
Without displaying superiority;
Without expecting acknowledgment;
Without causing trouble.

With every step the Divine Master took, we see him detachedly involved in continuous activity on behalf of the individual and the community.

From the carpenter's shop in Nazareth to the cross in Jerusalem, he spreads the Good without any payment other than the joy of doing his Father's Will.

He extols the widow's mite and praises Zacchaeus' fortune with the same serenity.

He talks lovingly with children and multiplies the loaves for thousands of people without changing who he was.

He raises Lazarus from the tomb and walks to his doom with his attention focused on the Heavenly Designs.

Along the unending line of your days and hours, do not forget to act for the common good. However, so that illusion does strike you with the gall of disenchantment or loneliness, help everyone indiscriminately, and above all else, hold on to the glory of being useful, "so that the same sentiment may be in you as was in Jesus Christ."

~ 3 ~

On the Great Journey

By faith Abraham, being called, obeyed and went to a place he would receive as an inheritance, even though he did not know where he was going. — Paul. (Heb. 11:8)

By faith, disciples of the Gospel are called, like Abraham, to the sublime inheritance that is their destiny.

This calling reaches everyone.

The great Hebrew patriarch went without knowing where he was going…

And we, in turn, should also lift up our hearts and go.

We do not know the stops along the lengthy way, but we do know that our goal is Christ Jesus.

How many times will we be constrained to walk on the thornbushes of slander? How long will we tread the scabrous trail of incomprehension? How often will floods of tears smite our spirit? How many clouds will form between our thought and heaven on long stretches of the road?

It is impossible to say.

However, we must go always forward without discouragement on the internal pathway of our redemption.

Today, it is hard toil; tomorrow, it is responsibility; after that, suffering, and finally, loneliness...

Nevertheless, it is necessary to press on without getting discouraged.

If it is not possible to take two steps forward per day, let us advance a few inches, at least ...

The vanguard of new horizons of understanding, goodness, spiritual illumination and progress in virtue is open to us.

Let us climb the steep mountain without resting:

Defeating deserts...

Overcoming difficulties...

Piercing fogs...

Breaking down barriers...

Abraham obeyed without knowing where he was going and found the realization of his happiness.

Let us obey in turn, aware of our destination and convinced that the Lord is waiting for us beyond our cross, on the resplendent peaks of eternal resurrection.

~ 4 ~

Each One

Now, there is a diversity of gifts, but the Spirit is the same. – Paul. (1 Cor. 12:4)

In every place and situation, each one of us can display divine qualities for the edification of all those who are part of our lives.

Learning and teaching are ongoing tasks in which we can take part in increasing the common treasure of wisdom and love.

Those who administer can express fairness and magnanimity more often.

Those who obey can have more ample resources for demonstrating a job well-done.

The wealthy, better than anyone else, can do more work and share its blessings.

The poor have more latitude to cultivate the wealth of hope and dignity.

The strong can more easily be benevolent at any time.

The weak can be humble on any occasion without embarrassment.

The learned can help everybody with their expansive knowledge, hence renewing the general thought for the Good.

Learners, with their many opportunities, can always distribute the wealth of goodwill.

The healthy can practice charity far and wide.

The sick can more convincingly teach lessons of patience all around.

Thus, the gifts may be different, intelligence may be characterized by various levels, worthiness displays various qualities, and ability is the result of effort, but the Divine Spirit that sustains everyone is substantially the same.

All of us can accomplish much in our particular station in life.

Take a good look at your position and attend to the imperatives of the Infinite Good. Place above your own and the Divine Will will make use of you.

~ 5 ~

Can You Go?

"Come unto me…" – Jesus. (Mt. 11:28)

Believers hearken to the Master's call, heeding his blessed consolations. Spiritual instructors repeat it in order to communicate vibrations of spiritual comfort to their listeners.

Everyone listens to the words of Christ, who invites the troubled mind and the tormented heart to seek his refreshing embrace… However, if it is easy to hear and repeat the Lord's "Come unto me," how difficult the "Go to him" is!

Here, the Master's words are poured out like a vitalizing balm, but the bonds of immediate gratification are just too strong. There, the divine invitation is heard amidst promises of renewal for the redemptive journey, but the prison of discouragement isolates the spirit behind its unyielding bars. Yonder, the call of the Most High soothes the sorrows of the disillusioned soul, but breaking free from obstacles comprised of people and things, situations and seemingly pressing private interests is almost impossible.

Jesus, our Savior, opens his loving, compassionate arms to us. A life focused on him becomes enriched with imperishable values, and in the shade of his heavenly teachings, we press onward, through sanctifying toil, towards our Universal Homeland…

All believers may hear his consoling appeal, but very few show themselves to be valorous enough in the faith to go in search of his company.

In short, it is very pleasant to hear the "Come unto me."

However, can you truthfully say that you can go?

~ 6 ~

Accept the Correction

It is true that no discipline seems pleasant at the time; it seems painful. Later on, however, it produces the peaceable fruit of righteousness for those who have been trained by it. – Paul. (Heb. 12:11)

The soil is lacerated and torn under the pressure of the plough. However, it is not long until beautiful flowers and delicious fruit burst forth from its straightened furrows.

When pruned, the tree loses a lot of sap, becoming undernourished and ugly. However, in just a few weeks, it acquires new robustness, manifesting beauty and abundance.

The humble water leaves the comfort of the spring, undergoes the demands of movement, reaches the great river and then shares in the grandeur of the sea.

What occurs in the simple sphere of nature also occurs in the complex realm of the soul.

A correction is always hard, unpleasant and bitter; but for those who accept its instruction, it always results in the blessed fruits of experience, knowledge, understanding and righteousness.

The soil, the tree and the water must bear correction because they have no choice in the matter, but the human being, the champion of intelligence on the planet, is free to accept it and harbor it in his or her heart.

Hence, the problem of personal happiness will never be resolved by avoiding the reparative process.

Heavenly correction is obvious in every corner of the world.

However, very few accept its blessings, because most of the time such a gift does not come wrapped in ermine, and when raised to the lips, it does not taste like candy. It is clothed in thorns or mixed with gall under the guise of a curative and salutary medicine.

Therefore, do not waste your precious opportunity for improvement.

Toil and struggle, pain and obstacles are means of purification that we should make use of.

~ 7 ~

By Their Fruit

"By their fruit you shall know them." –
Jesus. (Mt. 7:16)

Not by its size;
Not by its shape;
Not by its branches;
Not by the magnificence of its crown;
Not by its green shoots;
Not by its dry foliage;
Not by its radiant look;
Not by its unpleasant appearance;
Not by its ancient trunk;
Not by its fragile leaves;
Not by its rough or smooth bark;
Not by its fragrant or odorless flowers;
Not by its attractive aroma;
Not by its repulsive smell;
　　No tree is known or admired for its outward appearance, but for its fruit, its usefulness, and its productivity.

The same is true of our spirit on its journey...

Nobody who is truly committed to the truth will testify on our behalf by what we seem to be, by the superficiality of our life, by the epidermis of our attitudes or individual expressions perceived en passant, but by the essence of our collaboration on the shared road of progress, by the weight of our concourse in the overall good.

"By their fruit you shall know them," said the Master.

"By our deeds we shall be known," we repeat.

~ 8 ~

Attentive Workers

But the one who always strives to abide by the perfect law of freedom, who does not neglect what he has heard but does it — he will be blessed in all that he does. — (James 1:25)

Above all else, disciples of the Good News — those who really follow the Master — understand their responsibilities and render sincere reverence to the law of liberty, knowing full well that they will reap what they have sown. They know that judges are held accountable to the court; administrators will answer for their duties; workers will be responsible for their obligations. And all persons working for progress and order, for the light and the good in their own situation, persevere in making use of the abilities they have received from Divine Providence, attentive to the lessons of the truth, and devoted to the good works entrusted to them by the Higher Powers of the earth.

Characterized by such attitudes, Christ's collaborators, whether statespersons or janitors, will be fulfilling their duty in the area in which they are to act and serve, as naturally as they interact with oxygen in the process of breathing.

If they are in a supervisory position, they do not wait for others to remind them about their responsibilities. If they are the ones being supervised, they do not need to be constantly told how to do their job. And of course, they will not expect the government to tell them it is time to fertilize their vegetable garden, nor will they expect decrees that require them to educate or improve themselves.

By strengthening their own freedom to learn, to improve themselves and to help others by means of total devotion to the worthy endeavors that society has entrusted to them, everything they do is blessed and begins to produce substantial prosperity and spiritual growth in their daily lives.

Such followers of the Gospel, such students of the Master, become attentive workers, entering, in glorious silence, the sublime ranks of the Heavenly Apostolate.

~ 9 ~

Let Us Be Content

But if we have food and clothing, let us be content with it. – Paul. (1 Tim. 6:8)

    Hoarders of wheat will furnish their table with but a few slices of bread to satisfy their hunger.
    Owners of textile factories will spare only a few square yards of fabric to make clothing for themselves.
    No one should feed or clothe themselves based on gluttony or vanity, but on the principles that govern life on its natural foundations.
    Why do you have to wait for a banquet to offer a few leftovers to those who are hungry?
    Why do you have to have a large sum of money first before assisting someone in want?
    Charity does not depend on one's wallet or purse. Its source is found in the heart.
    The desire to have enough money to help one's neighbor or oneself in times of uncertainty and insecurity is always

praiseworthy; however, limiting one's practice of the Good to a full coffer is deplorable.

Therefore, open the doors of your soul and allow your sentiment to shine on everyone, just like the sun, whose rays illuminate, comfort, nourish and warm…

The rain falls as mere drops but it fertilizes the soil and sustains billions of lives.

Let us share what little we may have, and amplified by love, with time it will turn into widespread prosperity.

If properly cared for, a few seeds may increase to eventually cover huge fields.

Thus, let us be joyful and help all those who are part of our journey, because, according to the wise words of the apostle, if we have the blessing of daily bread and clothing, we are to live and serve in peace and contentment.

～ 10 ～

Yes, Indeed

"Yes, indeed, I am coming soon." –
(Rev. 22:20)

Almost always, while human beings are still young, their attitude towards life is that of a child who is unaware of the value of time.

They think the days and nights are just too short for their happiness and thrilling adventures. A thousand enticements of ephemeral illusion obscure the way they see things, and time rushes by in a whirlwind of useless desires.

Rare are those who escape such a waste of time.

Usually, however, as they grow older and their soul has a relative degree of education, they quickly readjust their concept of time.

One week is just too short to accomplish what they need to do.

Whatever their situation, they now understand that the same endeavors are repeated – completely recapitulated – at certain months of the year, just like the seasons of winter and summer, of blossoming and fruit bearing, in the realm of nature.

Then, troubled and anxious, they do all they can to increase their efforts to fill their time or stretch it out.

And most often, at the end of the journey, when death takes them in the midst of their duties or entertainments, they have no chance to make up for the years they have wasted.

Therefore, do not allow yourself to be embroiled in the human jungle, unconcerned about your spiritual growth on the eternal pathway.

In the next to the last verse of the New Testament – that Letter of Divine Love for Humankind – the Lord made this solemn promise to the apostle: "Yes, indeed, I am coming soon."

So, use your time wisely and do not delay your preparation.

~ 11 ~

Let Us Glorify

To our God and Father be glory for ever and ever.
— Paul. (Phil. 4:20)

When the vase is taken out of the kiln, it says:
"Blessed be the heat that has made me hard."
When the plough is taken from the forge, it affirms:
"Blessed be the hammer that has shaped me."
When the polished piece of wood glows in the palace, it exclaims:
"Blessed be the blade that cut me cruelly, preparing me for beauty."
When silk shines in the temple, it says to itself:
"Blessed be the ugly silkworm that gave me life."
When the flower opens, velvety and sublime, it quickly gives thanks:
"Blessed be the dark soil that filled me with fragrance."
When the sick person recovers his health, he cries out happily:
"Blessed be the pain that taught me the lesson of balance."

Everything is beautiful; everything is great; everything is holy in God's house.

Let us thank the storm that renews, the struggle that perfects, and the suffering that enlightens.

The dawn is the wonder of heaven that comes after the night.

In all our difficulties and darkness, may our Father be glorified forever and ever.

~ 12 ~

Impediments

Let us set aside every impediment… and let us run with perseverance the race before us. – Paul. (Heb. 12:1)

Wherever you go, carrying the vessel of your faith and pouring it out in the form of good works, you will always encounter many impediments that make things difficult for you.

Today, it is the failure at your attempts to progress.

Tomorrow, it is the companion who fails you.

The day after, it is the unfair persecution of your ideal.

Then the day after that, it is the bitterness of bile coming from the lips of those who deserve your love.

From time to time, you have to endure other people's incomprehension.

Every now and then, you run up against a thousand obstacles that induce you to inertia or negativity.

Nevertheless, the journey ahead of us should unfold on the road of incessant good.

What are we to do with people and circumstances that hinder and immobilize us?

The Apostle to the Gentiles is categorical in his response:

"Let us set aside every impediment."

Setting difficulties aside, however, does not mean belittling other people's opinions when respectable, nor does it mean running from the daily struggle. It means respecting each person in whatever situation he or she may be; it means sharing the best angle in the good fight, with our best contribution to everyone's evolution. And in the innermost part of our heart, it means proceeding with Jesus today, tomorrow and always, acting and helping, learning and loving, until the Divine Light shines in our conscience as much as we are already inside it, albeit unconsciously.

~ 13 ~

Let Us Set Out

"I will rise and return to my father..." –
(Lk. 15:18)

When the prodigal son decided to return to his father's arms, he actually decided to rise inwardly.

To leave the dark cave of idleness and head for the field of regenerative action.

To get up off the cold ground of inertia and seek the heat of reconstructive activity.

To leave the valley of indecision and climb the mountain of spiritually constructive toil.

To escape the darkness and enter the light.

To leave his negative behavior behind and plunge into the reconstruction of his ideals.

He stood up and left for the Paternal Home.

However, prodigal sons and daughters of Life – such as we are – how many of us, after having failed at the most valuable opportunities, clamor for the Lord to help us in accordance with our unworthy desires so that we can be content and happy? How many of us have willingly descended into the abyss, and once in it, drowning in the dark current of our passions, beg for the presence of the Almighty through his messengers so that they may attend to our whims?

But if we are really committed to our self-improvement, let us stand on our own two feet and press forward.

Any improvement requires effort.

The view at the top requires climbing the mountain first.

If we aspire to a Higher Life, let us go forward following Jesus' standards.

"I will rise," said the young man in the parable.

Yes, let us rise.

~ 14 ~

An Opportune Question

And he asked them, "Did you receive the Holy Spirit when you believed?" (Acts 19:12)

    The Apostle's question still resounds in all directions and is highly opportune in the circles of Christianity.

    Everywhere, in the most varied situations, there are people who are just beginning to believe, and people who already do believe.

    Here, there are those who apparently accept the Gospel in order to be acceptable to those around them.

    There, there are those who search the fields of faith in order to resolve what they regard as important intellectual issues.

    Somewhere else, sick persons receive the help of charity and declare themselves to be followers of the Gospel because of the physical relief.

    Nevertheless, tomorrow most of them become as unhappy and desperate as they used to be.

    Such phenomena are very common in the arenas of Spiritism.

There are a large number of fellow Spiritists who claim to have faith because they confirmed the life-after-death of some discarnate family member, or because they were cured of a headache, or because they found solutions to certain problems in the physical struggle. However, tomorrow they still have doubts about spirit friends and respectable mediums; they develop new illnesses, or they get lost in new mazes of the human learning experience.

Paul's question is still current.

What kind of spirit have we received as a result of our belief in Jesus' guidance? The spirit of fascination? Of indolence? Of pointless scrutiny? Of constant disapproval of other people's lives?

If we do not harbor the spirit of sanctification, which makes us better individuals and renews us in Christ, then our faith is like a fragile candle, whose flame is easily extinguished by the first puff of wind.

~ 15 ~

Fraternity

"By this all men will know that you are my disciples: if you love one another." – Jesus. (Jn. 13:35)

Ever since Constantine's victory, which opened the doors of political hegemony to the Christian world, we have been through many experiences to show that we are disciples of Jesus.

We have held renowned councils, formulating daring conclusions regarding the nature of God, the Soul, the Universe and Life.

We have encouraged dreadful wars that imposed misery and terror on those who could not believe in the tenets of our faith.

We have fought over the tomb of the Divine Master by spreading ravenous fire and brandishing the murderous sword.

We have created commendams and religious posts by distributing poison and wielding the dagger.

We have lit fires for burnings at the stake, constructed gallows, invented tortures and built prisons for those who disagreed with our points of view.

We have encouraged insurrections that caused animosity between brothers and sisters in the name of the Lord, who, on the cross, bore witness of his devotion to all humankind.

We have built beautiful and sumptuous palaces and basilicas in his memory, forgetting that he did not have a stone on which to rest his head.

And today, we still nourish schism and discord, digging trenches of incomprehension and animosity against one another because we interpret the faith differently.

Nevertheless, the word of Christ is irrefutable.

We cannot claim to be wards of the Good News simply by our outward attitudes…

Yes, we do need education, which improves the mind; justice, which preserves order; material progress, which enriches work; and councils, which support the study of the faith. However, without the light of love all human activity may be lost in darkness…

We will be accepted as learners of the Gospel by cultivating the Kingdom of God, which begins in our inner life.

Therefore, let us extend pure and simple fraternity all around us by mutually helping one another … the fraternity that labors and assists, understands and forgives amid the humility and service that ensure the victory of the Good. Wherever we are, let us practice fraternity, recalling the word of the Lord, who clearly and surely asserted: "By this all men will know that you are my disciples: if you love one another."

~ 16 ~

Be Not Troubled

I found that the very commandment that was intended to bring life actually brought death.
– Paul. (Rom. 7:10)

If we were to ask the grain of wheat its opinion about the mill, it would, of course, say that the mill is a place of pure torment. Nonetheless, that is where the grain is transformed into the glory of the bread that feeds the world.

If we were to ask a piece of wood for its opinion about the saw, it would say that it is the cruel tool that dilacerates its entrails; even so, thanks to this supposed torturer, the wood becomes refined and useful for noble purposes.

If we were to ask the stone about the burin, it would certainly explain that it is an abominable persecutor of its peace-of-mind, wounding it day and night; however, it is due to its action that the stone is raised to the status of being one of earth's polished and gleaming treasures.

So it is with the soul. So it is with the struggle.

If we were to question people about the flesh, they would reply with a thousand absurdities. If we were to listen to them speak about suffering, we would hear old nonsense. If we were to ask them to say something about their problems, they would shed bitter tears.

Nevertheless, it is imperative to realize that from the body that has been disciplined by terrible obstacles and purifying suffering, the spirit always re-emerges more beautified, more robust and more enlightened for immortality.

Therefore, be not troubled before the struggle; instead, take a closer look.

What may seem like a failure is very often a victory, and what seems to contribute to your death is, in fact, a contribution to your progress in the eternal life.

~ 17 ~

Christ and Us

The Lord said to him in a vision, "Ananias!" And he answered, "Here I am, Lord." – (Acts 9:10)

Men and women wait for Jesus, and Jesus waits for them.

Do not think that the world can be redeemed unless souls are redeemed.

In order to spread the sublimity of his plan of salvation, the Master needs human hands to accomplish and strengthen it. He began his ministry by calling on the help of Peter and Andrew, and then he completed his group of twelve companions to initiate the work of planetary regeneration.

And, ever since the first day of the Good News, he has invited, called and asked for souls to come together in order to become instruments of his Divine Will, showing us that although redemption does come from the Most High, it will not materialize without the active collaboration of hearts of goodwill.

Even when he comes in person to ask someone to work in his field of light, as was the case in Paul's conversion, the Master still needs the collaboration of incarnate workers. After visiting the doctor from Tarsus, Jesus immediately went to Ananias and sent him to assist the new disciple.

Why was Jesus not concerned about following the new convert and assisting him in person? It was because, if men and women cannot become spiritually illumined and progress without Christ, by the same token, Christ cannot do without men and women in the work of uplifting and sublimating the world.

"Go and Preach."

"Behold, I send you."

"Shine your light before men."

"The harvest is great, but the harvesters are few."

Such statements by the Lord show the importance he places on the human contribution.

Let us love and work, purifying and serving always.

Wherever a follower of the Gospel is, that person is to be a messenger from the Heavenly Friend for the unending work of the Good.

Christianity means Christ and us.

~ 18 ~

Not Only

"Man does not live on bread alone." – Jesus. (Mt. 4:4)

Not only warm clothing that protects the body, but the shelter of higher knowledge that strengthens the soul.

Not only the comeliness of the physical face, but the beauty and nobleness of the sentiments as well.

Not only the eugenics that improves the muscles, but also the politeness that refines one's manners.

Not only the surgical procedure that extracts the organic defect, but also one's personal effort that annuls the soul's defect.

Not only the comfortable dwelling in which to live one's physical life, but also the invisible home of edifying principles, in which the spirit becomes useful, esteemed and respected.

Not only the honorable titles that decorate the transitory personality, but also the virtues that enrich the eternal conscience in the day-to-day struggle.

Not only light for one's mortal eyes, but also divine light for one's imperishable understanding.

Not only a pleasant appearance, but effective helpfulness as well.

Not only blossoms, but also fruit.

Not only ongoing teaching, but active exemplification as well.

Not only an excellent theory, but also sanctifying practice.

Not only ourselves, but others, too.

The Master said: "Man does not live on bread alone."

Let us apply this sublime concept to the immense arena of the world.

Good taste, harmony and dignity in one's outer life are a duty, but let us not forget the purity, the loftiness and the sublime resources of the inner life, with which we progress towards Eternity.

~ 19 ~

Feeding

"Feed my sheep." – Jesus. (Jn. 21:16)

The Divine Shepherd's request of Simon Peter's loving heart is highly significant for the continuance of his ministry.

Seeing humankind as his immense flock, Jesus does not tell Peter to use drastic measures to impose discipline.

No yelling or scolding;

No prisons or gallows;

No whips or rods;

No punishment or imposition;

No abandonment of unfortunates or flagellation of the wayward;

No lamentation or despair.

"Peter, feed my sheep!"

That is to say: Brother, support those who are needier than you.

Do not let rebelliousness discourage you, nor condemn people's errors, from which a beneficial teaching will arise later on.

Help your neighbors instead of chastising them.

Teach always.

Be a faithful worker.

Be demanding of yourself, and support the infirm and fragile hearts that follow in your footsteps.

If you sow the Good, time will take care of the germination, growth, blossoming and fructification at the right moment.

Do not criticize, thus destroying.

A novitiate today may be a mentor tomorrow.

Support your neighbor's "good side" and go forward. Life will transform all evil into rubbish and the Lord will do the rest.

~ 20 ~

Difference

You believe there is only one God: you do well! The demons also believe, and tremble.
– (James 2:19)

The apostle's warning is of essential importance in the area of spiritual counsel.

Expecting benefits from heaven is an attitude common to all of us.

Worshiping the Lord can be the endeavor of both the just and the unjust.

Believing in the existence of the Divine Government is a prevailing characteristic of all people.

Believing in the Supreme Power is proper to good and bad persons alike.

James was divinely inspired in this verse because his words define the difference between merely believing in God and in carrying out his Sublime Will.

Intelligence is an attribute of everyone.

Knowledge comes from experience.

Human beings are always evolving and those who evolve learn and know.

The difference between good spirits and bad ones lies in the way they use their knowledge.

"Demons" – symbols of wickedness – satisfies their own desires, which are often insane and dark.

"Angels" identify with the designs of the Eternal One and comply with them wherever they may be.

Therefore, remember that when it comes to the issue of your personal happiness, your religious affiliation will not be enough by itself.

Worshiping God, and hoping and believing in Him are characteristic of all peoples.

The only sign that can reveal your nobler condition will be the way you live your life as you fulfill his designs, because actually, simply believing in the good that comes from the Lord will not do much for your spiritual growth. It takes due diligence in practicing the Good today, here and now, in his name.

~ 21 ~

Greatness

...The lesser is blessed by the greater. –
Paul. (Heb. 7:7)

In any activity in life there are those who reach natural greatness amongst their relatives, friends and contemporaries.

There are those who are great because of their knowledge, virtue or competence.

In general, however, those who are elevated to any level of superiority usually use their status to neglect their debt to regular people.

Those who become financially great often become avaricious; those who stand out as scientists become conceited; and those who come into power embrace vain pride.

However, the Law of Life does not allow for exclusivism or separatism.

According to the divine principles, all true progress is to become a blessing for the whole community.

Nature itself offers sublime lessons in this regard.

A tree grows to bear fruit.

A spring grows to benefit the soil.

If you have grown in experience or have reached a higher position of some kind, remember fraternal communion with all.

The sun, with its rays of light, does not abandon the muddy cavern or scorn the worm.

Growth is power.

Mind how you use the advantages you have been given in life. The Greatest Spirit of all those who have ever been born accepted offering the ultimate sacrifice in order to help all unconditionally.

Do not forget that according to the Divine Statute, the "lesser is blessed by the greater."

～ 22 ～

The Reward

Peter said to him: "We have left everything to follow you! What, then, will there be for us?"
– (Mt. 19:27)

The apostle's question expresses the attitude of many souls regarding their religion.

Someone devotes him or herself to a certain circle of faith and immediately asks: "What's in it for me?"

The answer, however, comes silently through the course of his or her own life.

What does the ripened grain receive after the harvest?

The mill that helps refine it.

What reward is given to the white, purified flour?

The yeast that transforms it for general usefulness.

What is the loaf's reward after being baked?

The blessing of being of service.

Christians are not made to be living adornments for the world, but to help regenerate and sanctify life.

Long ago, when kings and queens received the spoils of the defeated, they would use them to surround themselves with gratifications of a physical nature, with which they hastened their death.

In Christ, however, the picture is otherwise.

In him, we are victorious as we become brothers and sisters of all of those who share life with us, bearing in mind the obligation to be helpful and useful to them.

Simon Peter, who wanted to know what his reward would be for following the Gospel, experienced, firsthand, the need for self-sacrifice. The more he grew in faith, the greater the testimonies of love for humankind that were required of him. The more knowledge he acquired, the more the charity that was expected of him up till the ultimate sacrifice.

Thus, if due to your devotion to Jesus you have broken the bonds that used to hold you to the lower levels of life, remember that, for your happiness, heaven has given you the honor of helping, the privilege of understanding and the glory of serving.

~ 23 ~

Before the Sublime

Do not regard as common what God has purified. – (Acts 10:15)

There are expressions in the Gospel, which, like flowers attached to a divine branch, should be taken from their context so that we may marvel before their individual brightness and fragrance.

The voice from heaven that speaks to Simon Peter in Acts entails horizons that are much broader than the apostle's personal issues.

Regular individuals are surrounded by earth's glories; even so, they think everything is ordinary; they are incapable of valuing the richness around them.

Blind before the superb spectacle of life that frames their development, they trample on the treasures of the world without thinking about the patient effort of the centuries that Infinite Wisdom has taken to perfect and select the qualities that surround them.

How many millennia were needed to shape a rock?

How many elements are harmonized to form a simple ray of sunlight?

How many obstacles were overcome so that the flower could materialize?

How much effort was necessary to domesticate certain animals and trees?

How many centuries did it take for the Patience of Heaven to build the complex structure of the human body in which the incarnate spirit is manifested?

Before the sublime, reason is a gradual light.

My brothers and sisters, do not forget that the Lord has placed you in a veritable paradise for you earthly experience, a paradise where the tiny seed can produce enormous quantities, and where flowers and water, soil and atmosphere invite you to work for the increase of the Eternal Treasures.

So, each and every day, praise the Lord, who has provided you with precious opportunities and divine gifts…

Think, study, toil and serve.

Do not regard as common what God has purified and ennobled.

~ 24 ~

By Their Works

Hold then in highest esteem and love because of their work. — Paul. (1Thess. 5:13)

This verse from Paul's First Epistle to the Thessalonians is particularly important for our daily struggle.

We all tend to devote more esteem to those who see life from our own point of view. Our love is always warmest for those who espouse our own ways of seeing things, our engrained habits and our social principles; nevertheless, our interpretations are not always the best; our habits are not always the most commendable, nor are our principles always the most praiseworthy.

Thus, we must disintegrate the shell of our selfishness in order to dedicate our friendship and respect to our brothers and sisters, not because of their emotional link to our personal itinerary, but because of their faithfulness to the common good.

If we love someone solely because of his or her physical attractiveness, tomorrow we will likely find that the object of our affection is on the way to the scrap heap.

If we hold someone in esteem solely for his or her brilliant oratory, it is possible that he or she may lose his or her voice sometime soon.

If we are devoted to someone only because he or she blindly obeys us, we may be causing that person to make the same mistakes that we have made so many times.

It is essential that we improve our perceptions and feelings so that we may progress on the road to a superior life.

Above all, let us seek the company of others because of the works with which they benefit the space and time in which we live, since there will come a day when we understand that the best companion is seldom the one who agrees with us, but is always the one who agrees with the Lord and collaborates with him to make life better inside and outside of us.

~ 25 ~

Concerning Christ's Gifts

But grace has been given to each one of us according to the measure of the gift of Christ.
– Paul. (Eph. 4:7)

Over these twenty centuries of Christianity, the human soul has been a consciousness enlightened by reason amidst a battle for acquiring illuminative personal qualities.

The battlefield is to be found within our inner life.

Animality versus spirituality.

Millennia of deep-set darkness against the nascent light.

And human beings, between the alternatives of life and death, being reborn in the physical body and returning to the spirit life, little by little shape the sublime inner qualities that are essential for their spiritual ascension, and which, in fact, constitute the progressive virtues of Christ in each one of us.

That is why Divine Grace occupies human existence or grows within it, insofar as the incipient, small, regular or great gifts of Jesus are expressed in it.

Wherever you may be, or whoever you may be, seek to develop Christian qualities within you, with the same watchful attention that is given to cultivating precious plants in the home.

As for the earth, we are all susceptible to engender good or evil.

Let us offer the vessel of our hearts to the Divine Cultivator, bearing in mind that if the "conscious soil" of our spirit accepts his seeds, then each crumb of our goodwill will most certainly become a miraculous channel for the exteriorization of the Good, with the ongoing multiplication of the gifts of the Lord all around us.

Observe your "good side" and remember you can increase it infinitely.

Do not try to destroy millennia of darkness all at once.

Strive for self-improvement each and every day.

Persevere in learning from the Master of Love and Selflessness.

Let us not forget that Divine Grace will fill our personal space according to our real growth in the gifts of Christ.

~ 26 ~

A Worker without Faith

...and I will show you my faith by my works.
– (James 2:18)

Wherever we go, we will find workers who have no faith, spreading anxiety and discouragement.

They devote themselves to a certain charitable enterprise but abandon it soon after starting, saying: "What's the point? The world's not ready."

They commit themselves to ordinary endeavors, but in a display of lack of persistence, they abandon their spiritually constructive obligations, alleging: "I wasn't made for such demeaning servitude."

They get involved with a certain religion looking to enjoy its benefits, but they soon abandon it, saying: "All of this is a lie and a complication."

If they are invited to occupy an important position, they repeat the old refrain: "I don't deserve it! I'm unworthy."

When asked to endure a test of humility, they say with patent rebelliousness: "Who is offending me like this?"

And they go from one situation to the next between complaining and indiscipline, with a lot of time on their hands to feel persecuted and belittled.

These are the workers who do not finish the task that has been entrusted to them, or the students who study continuously without ever learning the lesson.

Do not get caught in a faith devoid of good works, for it is a dangerous inebriation of the soul; on the other hand, do not devote yourself to works without faith in the Divine Power and in your own efforts.

Workers who trust in the Law of Life realize that all the treasures and glories of the Universe belong to God. In view of this, they pass through this world under the light of enthusiasm and incessant work for the Good, completing their big and small endeavors without becoming vainly enamored with themselves or becoming enslaved to the creations of which they may have been valuable instruments.

Let us show our faith by means of our endeavors for everyone's happiness and the Lord will grant our lives the ineffable growth of love and wisdom, beauty and power.

27

Destruction and Misery

Destruction and misery mark their ways. –
Paul. (Rom. 3:16)

When disciples fail to trust in the Master and avoid acting according to the examples that his divine ministry bequeathed to us, preferring the broad pathway of infidelity to their own conscience, they dig deep abysses of destruction and misery wherever they go without even noticing it.

If their mind is crystalized in idleness, they destroy the goodwill in the hearts of the other workers around them and they restrain their own opportunities to serve.

If they go down the road of negativity, they destroy the tender hopes in the sentiments of those who are just starting out in the faith and they weave a vast net of darkness for themselves.

If they transfer their soul to the dark residence of vice, they smother their traveling companions' nascent virtues and they acquire heavy debts to be paid in the future.

If they give safe harbor to despair, they quench the tenuous light of trust within the soul of their neighbor and they weep in vain under the storm of destructive tears.

If they seek refuge in the cold house of depression, they asphyxiate the optimism of those who accompany them and they waste the wealth of time on fruitless complaining.

The Divine advice for the follower of the Gospel is to press on, helping, understanding and serving everybody.

Being inactive is to immobilize others and freeze oneself.

Being rebellious is to whip one's brothers and sisters and to hurt oneself.

To avoid the Good is to misguide others and nullify oneself.

Unfortunate are those who do not follow the Master once they have found him, because to know Jesus Christ in spirit and yet live far from him is to spread destruction all around us and to retain misery within us.

~ 28 ~

Something

"It is not the healthy who need a doctor, but the sick." – Jesus. (Lk. 5:31)

Those who know how to read should not neglect helping those who cannot.

Those who can express themselves clearly should teach others how to construct correct and expressive sentences.

Those who enjoy bodily health should seize the opportunity to assist the infirm.

Those who have managed to light a small torch of faith within their spirit should patiently support unfortunate persons who do not yet have the least notion of responsibility before the Lord, thus helping them overcome their inner darkness.

Those who have the means to work should not forget those who lack them, doing their best to help them find a worthy task.

Those who practice charity should have compassion on hardened souls, benefiting them with the vibrations of prayers.

Those who already value the treasure of humility should not avoid the proud, giving them a living example of the elements indispensable for inner change.

Those who have a good heart should not refuse to help those who do not, since badness invariably results from rebelliousness or ignorance.

Those who have found peace should support those who are desperate.

Those who possess joy should share their gift of contentment with the downhearted.

The Lord said that it is not the healthy who need a doctor, but the sick.

So, remember those who have bigger problems than yours.

Life does not demand that you sacrifice yourself completely for others, but for your own sake you should not pass up the opportunity to do something for the common good.

~ 29 ~

Let Us Serve

Serve willingly, as if you were serving the Lord and not men. – Paul. (Eph. 6:7)

If you legislate, but then do not abide by the Law according to the designs of the Lord, who considers the needs of all, you are walking on the edge of a dangerous abyss that you have dug with your erroneous creation, without reaping the benefits of your glorious mission in society.

If you administrate, but then do not bear in mind the interests of the Lord on the pathway on which you work as a steward of life, you run the risk of burying your heart in dark desires, without reaping the fruits of the function you perform in the public ministry.

If you judge your neighbor, but do not model yourself after the Lord, who knows all the details and circumstances of every lawsuit in court, then you may face the possibility of falling spectacularly into the same hole as those you have hastily judged, without benefiting from the gifts of wisdom that Justice maintains in your mind.

Whether you work with colors or marble, with words or songs, but do not bring the love and the light of the Lord into your work as you should, then you are assuming the huge responsibility of those who produce the wrong sort of images for the popular consumer mind, thus you miss out on the glory that could enrich your sentiments.

If you are supposed to obey others in order to be useful to the world, but you do not do so with the spirit of understanding as taught by the Lord, who helped people and loved them even to the point of personal sacrifice, then you are living amidst the ghosts of indiscipline and discouragement, without fulfilling the divine light of the talent that lies in your hands.

Dear friend, the time you have on the earth is a sublime learning experience.

Work is always the instructor of spiritual growth.

Let us serve without attachments.

In every place in the human valley, there are resources for improvement and action for those who want to evolve. Let us serve willingly wherever we may be, as if we were serving the Lord and not merely other people, and he will lead us to the higher realms of life.

~ 30 ~

Educate

Do you not know that you are God's temple and that God's Spirit lives in you?
– Paul. (1 Cor. 3:16)

Inside the tiny seed lives the blueprint of the whole tree.
In the heart of the soil are melodies of the spring.
In blocks of stone are the masterpieces of statuary.
Nonetheless, the orchard needs constant care.
The crystal clear spring needs an aqueduct so that it may run without becoming contaminated.
The sculptured stone requires the work of the chisel.
Similarly, the spirit harbors the gene of Divinity.
God is in us as much as we are in God.
However, so that the divine light may shine forth from human darkness, it is necessary for the educational processes of life to work in us on the stony pathway of the millennia.
Only the heart ennobled in great understanding can pour forth a sanctifying heroism.

Only the educated mind can produce illuminated forms of thought.

Only spiritual greatness can produce a soothing voice to speak balanced, sublime words.

Let us understand pain and toil as the heavenly artists of our spiritual purification.

Educate and you will transform irrationality into intelligence; intelligence into humanity and humanity into angelhood.

Educate and you will build heaven on earth.

Since we know that the Lord dwells in us, let us improve our lives so that we may reflect him.

~ 31 ~

Farmers

The hardworking farmer should be the first to enjoy the fruits of the harvest. – Paul. (2 Tim. 2:6)

There are farmers of every kind.

There are those who buy the land and develop it using the efforts of hardworking tenants, without ever touching the soil with their own hands.

There are many farmers who abandon the plow to rust, crossing their arms and blaming the rain or the sun for the failure of the harvest.

There are farmers who keep a watch on their neighbor's crops, but pay no attention to their own.

Many speak disproportionately about a thousand things that really do not matter, while destructive worms wipe out the fragile plants.

There are many who complain that the soil is incapable of producing anything, but they have neglected giving the blessing of water and fertilizer to the field that has been entrusted them.

Many complain of headaches, colds or other physical indispositions, and they lose out on the sublime opportunity to sow.

Nature repays all of them with disillusionment, difficulties, failure and disappointment.

Nevertheless, the farmer who works hard soon receives the blessing of a full barn.

And so it goes with the farming of the spirit.

Nobody can obtain excellent results without putting forth an effort, devoting the best they have to offer to the work of the Good.

Writing in a time of landowners and slaves, of superficiality and favoritism, Paul of Tarsus does not say that the wealthier sower or the one favored by Caesar would be the actual owner of the harvest, but he did rightly say that the farmer who devoted himself to his obligations would be the first to enjoy the fruits of the harvest.

~ 32 ~

The Good Part

"Mary has chosen the good part, and it will not be taken from her." – Jesus. (Lk. 10:42)

Do not forget the "good part" that resides in everyone and everything.

The fire may destroy, but it also brings the purifying element.

The stone may bruise, but it also consolidates security.

The gale may lash mercilessly, but it also helps to bring renewal.

The torrent may be dirty, but it brings the fertilizer indispensable for a successful planting.

Likewise, there are persons who are useless in certain aspects of the human struggle, whereas they are extremely valuable in others.

A unilateral judgment is always ruinous.

There is neither complete imperfection nor complete perfection on this plane of evolution.

The criminal condemned by everyone today may be the healthcare giver who gives you a glass of water tomorrow.

The person in whom you discern a trace of darkness may later turn out to be the enlightened brother or sister who gives you a worthy example to follow.

The tempest of the times in which we live at the moment very often becomes the fount of wellbeing in the time we have left to us.

Let us look for the positive side of situations, events and persons.

"Mary has chosen the good part, and it will not be taken from her," said the Lord.

Let us assimilate the essence of this divine lesson.

In the field of life, those who look for the "good part" and seek harbor in it receive the spiritual treasure that will never be taken from them.

~ 33 ~

Raising and Helping

And taking her by the hand, he helped her up.
– (Acts. 9:41)

    This lesson from Acts, in which Peter brings Dorcas back to life, is very significant.

    The apostle is not content with saying beautiful things in her ears, so as to restore her general energies.

    No, he takes her by the hand and helps her up.

    The teaching is highly symbolic.

    We often see people helped up in knowledge, joy and virtue, bathed in the divine light of the Master, and who are then able to help thousands of people up to the Higher Realms.

    However, preaching alone is not enough to do so.

    Sermons are actually sublime appeals, and Christ himself used them. Still, we must not forget that although the Heavenly Friend taught on the mount, he also multiplied the loaves there for the hungry people, thus re-strengthening their enthusiasm.

We, who, in the past, were dead in ignorance, and who, today – thanks to the Infinite Mercy – already enjoy some blessings of light, need to reach out to others.

However, we cannot shirk our saving endeavor by simply giving a few admirable sermons.

We have to use our hands in working for the Good.

And using our hands means getting involved personally.

Unless we use our energies to help Christ build the Spiritual Kingdom on earth, it will do no good for us to proclaim excellent words about the treasures of the Good News or about the need for human redemption.

If we find brothers or sisters fallen down on the way, let us do all we can to awaken them with the resources of the transforming word, but let us also remember that, in order to bring them back to a constructive life, according to Peter's unforgettable lesson, we will have to reach out fraternally to them.

~ 34 ~

Let us be Alert

...but nothing is pure to those who are corrupted and do not believe. – Paul. (Titus 1:15)

People always see by means of their internal sight.

By the colors they use on the inside, they judge aspects on the outside.

They determine other people's feelings by their own.

In the conduct of others, they think they can find the means and ends that concern their own actions.

Hence the imperative need for constant vigilance, so that our conscience is not contaminated by evil.

When darkness takes over our mind, we see nothing but darkness everywhere.

In expressions of the purest love, we imagine carnal allusions.

If we meet a friend dressed with commendable refinement, vanity comes to mind.

If one of our friends is called to a career in politics, we visualize political abuse.

If one of our neighbors has perfect timing regarding his or her investment, we suspect misappropriation.

When a friend is vigorously defending a just cause, we immediately classify him or her as intractable.

When darkness is allowed to enter our inner life, deplorable changes may reach our thoughts.

In such circumstances, virtues are never noticed.

Evil, however, is always abundant.

Generous acts of beneficence are wrongly interpreted.

Let us be alert every time we are visited by envy, jealousy, suspicion or slander.

There are intricate situations for which silence is a blessed and effective medicine, because each spirit sees the pathway or the trekker in accordance with its light or dark inner sight.

ns 35 ns

Let Us Spread the Good

Do not be overcome by evil, but overcome evil with good. — Paul. (Rom. 12:21)

When facing evil, all the elements of nature do all they can to restore harmony and ensure the victory of the Good.

When a storm seems to have destroyed the landscape, the divine forces of life come together to restore it.

The sun shines on the slough, healing the wounds of the soil.

The wind caresses the grove, drying out the branches.

The song of the birds replaces the voice of the thunder.

The plain receives the run-off without complaining and transforms it into precious fertilizer.

The air, which bore the weight of the clouds and the shock of the destructive lightning, becomes light and pleasant.

The tree with broken or damaged fronds regenerates itself in silence so as to produce new blossoms and new fruit.

The earth, our common mother, has to endure mudslides and hailstorms periodically, but it does not cease to enrich the Good more and more each day.

In view of this, why do we harbor the bile and bitterness of evil in our heart?

Let us learn to cope with adversity, educating its energies to improve our lives.

Ignorance is merely a long night that eventually gives way to the sun of wisdom.

Use the treasure of your love in all directions and spread the Good everywhere you go.

Even when deluged with silt, the spring does not give up. It just receives it and transforms it into blessings as it gently and humbly flows along to everyone's benefit.

~ 36 ~

Clarifying Affirmation

"Yet you do not want to come to me and live."
– Jesus. (Jn. 5:40)

All those who strive for the sublimation of the individuality need to understand the supreme value of the will in their spiritual growth.

The churches and schools of Christianity are full of learners who glimpse Jesus' divine powers and recognize his magnanimity, but experience strong vacillations, nevertheless.

They believe and disbelieve; they help and refuse to help; they organize and disorganize; they are illuminated by the faith and let distrust darken their spirit...

This is because they expect the Lord to take care of their immediate physical needs, but they do not want to go to him to grasp life eternal.

They ask for miracles from Christ's hands, yet they do not accept his precepts. They ask for his consoling presence, yet they do not follow in his footsteps. They love to listen to him on the edge of the serene lake as he preaches hope and comfort, yet they refuse to share the toil of the streets with him through sacrifice for the victory of the Good. They flatter him with flowers in Jerusalem, yet they avoid showing goodness and understanding before the frantic and sickly multitude. They ask him for the blessings of the resurrection, yet they hate the cross of thorns that regenerates and sanctifies.

They could be part of the edifying vanguard, yet they do not want to be.

They clamor for the divine light, yet they are afraid to forsake the darkness.

They yearn for better conditions in life, yet they detest the idea of having to renew themselves.

Thus, we can see that it is easy to eat the loaves multiplied by the infinite love of the Divine Master or rejoice in his healing power, but in order to experience the Abundant Life, of which he is the sublime ambassador, simply wanting and believing are not enough. The persevering will of having learned to toil, serve and grow spiritually are also needed.

In the Regenerative Work

Brothers, if one of you is caught in sin, you who are spiritual should guide him with a spirit of gentleness, watching yourselves so that you, too, are not tempted. – Paul (Gal. 6:1)

If we use expressions of anger to try to guide brothers or sisters who are lost in the entanglement of error, all we will do is awaken their own anger against us.

If we strike them with blows, they will retaliate with many more against us.

If we point out their wrongs, they might point out our own.

If we think they ought to suffer the same evil that they have inflicted on another, then we are just increasing the evil around us.

But if we encourage their wrongful behavior, we are approving the wrong.

If we remain indifferent, we are supporting the disturbance.

However, if we deal with their error as someone who wants to heal a sick friend, then we are manifesting the regenerative work.

In difficult times, when we see persons caught in inner darkness, we should remember that if we want to help them, it is as unwise to criticize them as it is to praise them.

If one cannot put out a fire by throwing gasoline on it, one cannot heal wounds by applying perfume on them.

Let us be humane before anything else.

Let us approach unfortunate persons with understanding and fraternity.

We will not lose anything if we exercise the respect we owe to everyone and everything.

Let us put ourselves in the accused person's shoes and remind ourselves that if we had been in the same situation, we might not have resisted the suggestions of evil either. Let us analyze our advantages and his or her disadvantages with impartiality and good intentions.

Every time we proceed in this way, the situation changes in the smallest aspects.

Otherwise, it will always be easy to scold and condemn, yet fall into the same wrong ourselves when we are visited by the same temptation.

~ 38 ~

If We only Knew

"Father, forgive them, for they do not know what they are doing." – Jesus. (Lk. 23:34)

If murderers knew beforehand how much pain life is going to charge them in order to readjust their destiny, they would prefer not to even have arms at all in order to withhold the deadly blow.

If defamers could eliminate the crust of darkness that maddens their vision and foresee the suffering that awaits them as they settle accounts with the truth, they would paralyze their vocal cords or lay down their pen rather than wrongly accuse someone.

If deserters of the Good could see the dangerous traps that the darkness sets to steal their joy of living, they would gladly wear the sanctifying shackles of the heaviest responsibilities.

If ingrates could see the bile of bitterness that will invade their heart later on, they would never perpetrate the crime of indifference.

If selfish persons could perceive the infernal loneliness that is waiting for them, they would never depart from the tireless practice of fraternity and cooperation.

If gluttons could see the damage they are causing their body, thus hastening their death, they would render unwavering worship to frugality and harmony.

If we knew how terrible the result of disrespecting the Divine Laws will be, we would never depart from the upright road.

So, forgive those who hurt you or slander you…

Those who give in to the disturbing suggestions of evil do not know what they are doing.

~ 39 ~

Inoperative Faith

In the same way, faith without works is dead.
(James 2:17)

Inoperative faith is a problem that has always required utmost attention so that the disciple of the Gospel may clearly grasp the fact that the noblest ideal, without the work that manifests it in benefit of others, will always be a lovely yet unproductive landscape.

What would we say about a powerful motor that is never used by anyone, a spring that is never used to water a field, or a lamp that never gives off light?

We may be confident about a certain seed, but if we do not go ahead and plant it, what result can we expect from it except mere uselessness? We know that a plank of lumber can be used for many good purposes, but if we do not use the saw or plane on it, it will eventually rot away.

Religious faith is the means.

Ministry is the end.

Heavenly trust illuminates the mind so that beneficent activity may result from it, spreading blessings of peace and joy, ennoblement and sublimation all around.

Those who can receive just one drop of spiritual knowledge in the core of their soul, demonstrating the maturity needed for the superior life, should immediately look for the service to which they are called for everyone's progress.

Essentially, faith is like the mustard seed of Jesus' teachings, which, as it grows taller by means of incessant work, becomes the Divine Kingdom, where the believer's soul begins to live.

Therefore, to keep religious ecstasy in the heart without doing any work to develop wisdom and love, which are part of the service of charity and education, is the same as keeping in the living soil of the sentiment a dead idol buried amongst useless flowers of shining promises.

~ 40 ~

Concerning the Objective

And somehow to attain to the resurrection. –
Paul (Phil. 3:11)

We will achieve the goal we keep in view.

Misers dream of a safe full of money and achieve it.

Malefactors usually spend a long time planning a crime and then commit it.

Astute politicians long for authority and finally reach a high position in the earthly realm.

Imprudent women who focus their thoughts on misusing their emotions enter the land of troubling self-indulgences.

Every goal has its price.

To amass wealth, misers almost always surrender their peace-of-mind.

When they commit a crime, criminals dishonor their name.

In order to reach the position of power, opportunists very often ruin their character.

In their search for fanciful pleasures, injudicious women usually abdicate their right to be happy.

If such heavy burdens are imposed on those who pursue completely inferior goals in the physical realm, what tribute will the spirit who pursues the glory of the life eternal have to pay?

The Master on the cross is the answer to everyone who pursues the sublimity of resurrection.

By keeping his eye on this goal, Paul was able to pursue it, in spite of the incomprehension of others, whippings, afflictions and stonings as he unswervingly served in the name of the Lord.

Therefore, if you desire to reach the same destination, focus your aspirations on the sanctifying objective and go forward, making a valiant effort to win the eternal reward.

~ 41 ~

On the Difficult Road

"I will never leave you, nor forsake you."
(Heb. 13:5)

The Word of the Lord does not refer only to sustaining one's physical life on the stony climb of the ascent.

Much more than food for the body, we need food for the spirit.

The cells of the body may experience hunger and clamor for ordinary soup, but the necessities and wishes, impulses and emotions of the soul often cause immeasurable afflictions, demanding ampler spiritual nourishment.

There are times when our innermost reserves are profoundly depleted.

Our strength seems exhausted and our hopes retreat in apathy. Darkness invades our soul, as if we were enveloped in dark night.

And as happens to nature under the mantle of night, even though we have springs of understanding and flowers of goodwill in the vast expanse of our inner world, everything remains veiled by the fog of our troubles.

However, even then the All-Merciful does not abandon us completely to the darkness of our doubts and disappointments. Just as he makes effulgent stars shine in the sky, unveiling a constellated pathway of the firmament to the traveler lost in the world, he also lights the fire of new convictions and loftier aspirations in the sky of our ideals so that our spirit does not get lost on its journey toward the higher life.

"I will never leave you, nor forsake you," promises the Divine Goodness.

Neither loneliness, nor abandonment.

Heavenly Providence continues watching over us…

Therefore, let us hold to the comforting certainty that every storm is followed by a tranquil atmosphere, and that there is never a night without the dawn.

42

For a Short Time

Instead, choosing to be mistreated as one of God's people rather than to enjoy sin for a short time. – Paul. (Heb. 11:25)

In this verse, Paul refers to Moses' attitude of abstaining from enjoying the luxuries of Pharaoh's house for a short time in order to devote himself to liberating his compatriots from captivity, thereby creating a sublime image that defines the position of the spirit that has incarnated on the earth.

"For a short time" an administrator guides people's interests.

"For a short time" a servant obeys in a position of subordination.

"For a short time" a usurer holds on to his or her money.

"For a short time" an unfortunate person endures hardships.

Ah! If people would only realize how short are their days on earth! If they could only see how precarious are the resources they depend on in the vessel of their flesh!

Such a perception in light of eternity would certainly give them a new concept of the blessed, invaluable, yet short opportunity that has been given to them.

Everything benefits or afflicts the human being for just a short while.

Nevertheless, many people use this tiny fraction of time to complicate their lives for many years.

It is essential to focus one's mind and heart on the example of those who were able to glorify their brief pilgrimage on the day-to-day pathway.

Moses gave up the enjoyment of Pharaoh's household "for a short time" so that he could leave us the righteous law.

Jesus did not dare complain even "for a short time" in face of the cruelty of those who persecuted him, so as to teach us the divine secret of the Cross and Eternal Resurrection.

Paul did not rest even "for a short time" after meeting the Master at the gates of Damascus, so that he could bequeath us his example of toil and living faith.

My friend, wherever you are, remember that you will be there only "for a short time." Use moderation in times of joy and resign yourself in times of sadness, toiling incessantly to spread the, for it is how you use the "short time" that will determine how you proceed to the "long time" of either happiness or suffering.

~ 43 ~

Language

Wholesome and blameless language so that our adversaries may be ashamed, having nothing bad to say about us. – Paul. (Titus 2:8)

It is through their language that people either help or harm themselves.

Even when our soul is fogged over with problems, it is not advisable for our speech to be cloudy or imbalanced toward others.

We all have our enigmas, our necessities and our suffering, and it is not right to increase our neighbor's afflictions with the burden of our own.

Complaining openly causes discouragement; bitter words are like a whipping; the defamer's remark confuses...

By criticizing people when they err, we are keeping the truth away from us.

By using demeaning words, we repel the blessings of love that would fill us with the joy of living.

Let us have the courage needed to eliminate, by ourselves, the expressions of our uncontrolled sentiments and desires.

Speech is the channel of the "self."

Through the outlet of the tongue, our passions may explode or our virtues may be spread.

Every time we express the vocabulary that characterizes us, we emit energies that may destroy or build up, that ruin or restore, that hurt or soothe.

In our opinion, language is comprised of three essential elements: expression, manner of speaking and tone of voice.

If we do not make our phrasing clear; if we do not purify the manner in which we speak; and if we do not discipline our voice according to the situation, we are susceptible of missing out on the best opportunities of self-improvement, understanding and spiritual growth.

Paul of Tarsus provides the appropriate recipe to students of the Gospel.

One's language should be neither too sweet, nor too bitter; neither too mild, which would drive trust away, nor too harsh or bruising, which would ruin affinity. Instead, we should use "… wholesome and blameless language so our adversaries may be ashamed, having nothing bad to say about us."

~ 44 ~

Let Us Have Faith

"I go to prepare a place for you." —
Jesus. (Jn. 14:2)

The Master knew that, until his Divine Kingdom was built on earth, all those who followed him could be seen as misplaced people, working for everyone's moral progress but without a proper "place" for their sublime ideals.

In fact, loyal Christians are seldom treated with due respect, no matter where they go.

Since they are almost always out of step with partially-Christianized society, they have to endure the uncharitable opinions of many.

If they practice humility, they are called cowards.

If they adopt a simple life, they are called unambitious.

If they try to be benevolent, they are labeled as fools.

If they administer worthily, they are judged as proud.

If they obey when it is right to do so, they are considered servile.

If they apply tolerance, they are seen as incompetent.

If they show firmness, they are cruel.

If they work industriously, they are seen as vain.

If they strive for self-improvement, assuming responsibilities in an intensive effort to do good works or to engage in consoling conversations, people think they are just pretending.

If they try to help their neighbor, approaching the multitude with gestures of spontaneous goodness, they are accused of being egocentric and opportunist, seeking their own interests.

But in spite of such conflicts, let us continue working and serving in the name of the Lord.

Recognizing that the home of his followers is not built on the soil of the world, Jesus promised to prepare a place for them in the higher realms.

Therefore, let us double our efforts at sowing the Good as laborers who are temporarily distant from their true home.

"In my Father's house there are many mansions."

And Christ keeps on serving, ahead of us.

Let us have faith.

~ 45 ~

Only in this Way

"In this is my Father glorified: that you bear much fruit; thus you will be my disciples." – Jesus. (Jn. 15:8)

In our times of affliction, the Father is invoked.
In times of joy, he is worshiped.
On stormy nights, he is anxiously longed for.
On festive days, he is solemnly revered.
Praised by his thankful children and forgotten by ingrates, the Father always gives, spreading the blessings of his infinite goodness amongst the good and the bad, the just and the unjust.

He teaches the worm to crawl, the bush to grow and the human being to think.

Nonetheless, no one should have any doubts about what the Supreme Lord expects of us. From one lifetime to the next, he helps us to grow and to serve him so that someday we may become part of his divine Love and glorify him.

However, we will never arrive at such a condition simply by means of a thousand bright hues of sentiments and reasoning.

Our higher ideals are indispensable, and at heart they resemble the most beautiful and fragrant flowers of a tree. Our learning is essential, of course, and in essence it comprises the robustness of the respectable trunk. Our lofty aspirations are precious and necessary and they represent the living and promising leaves.

All these requirements are imperative for the harvest.

The same happens in the fields of the soul.

Only when we open ourselves to the Father's decrees of universal love, working for the eternal Good, can we glorify him.

To that end, the Master was clear in his statement.

May our activity on life's journey produce much fruit of peace and wisdom, love and hope, faith and joy, justice and mercy, in a constant and worthy personal endeavor, for that is the only way we can glorify the Father, and the only condition in which we can be disciples of the Crucified and Resurrected Master.

~ 46 ~

On the Cross

"He saved others but could not save himself."
– (Mt. 27:42)

Yes, he had redeemed many…

He had spread love and truth, peace and light; he had healed the sick and had resurrected the dead.

Nevertheless, he himself had been lifted up on a cross between thieves.

In fact, for someone who had been praised so much, who had reached the pinnacle, indirectly suggesting his status as Redeemer and King, the fall was enormous…

He was the Prince of Peace and was defeated by the war of inferior interests.

He was the Savior, yet did not save himself.

He was the Just One, yet suffered the ultimate injustice.

There hung the Lord, flogged and defeated.

According to human consensus, it was the ultimate loss.

He had fallen on the cross.

He was bleeding, but upright.

He was tortured, but his arms were outstretched.

He was relegated to suffering, but suspended from the earth.

Surrounded by hatred and sarcasm, he kept his heart filled with love.

He had fallen, vilified and forgotten, but on another day he transformed his suffering into divine glory. His head had hung down, covered in blood on the cross, yet he arose in a garden in the light of the sun.

The dark defeat was transformed into resplendent victory. The offensive wood was covered with heavenly light for the whole earth.

Such is the case in our own lives.

Do not stumble on the easy triumph or the cheap halo of crucifiers. Every time circumstances compel you to change course in your life, take the way of self-sacrifice, transforming your pain into benefit for many, because all those who accept the cross on behalf of their brothers and sisters find the way to resurrection eternal.

~ 47 ~

Self-Liberation

*For we brought nothing into this world,
and we can take nothing when we leave it*
– Paul (1 Tim. 6:7)

If you wish to free your soul from the dark chains of the "ego," then start your course of self-liberation by learning to live "as if possessing everything, yet having nothing," "with everyone, yet without anyone."

Since you arrived in this world as a pilgrim needing shelter and help, and since you know that you will leave it alone, then resign yourself to living with yourself, serving everyone for the sake of your spiritual growth towards immortality.

Remember that, due to the laws that rule our destinies, each person is or will be all by him or herself in his or her own way, acquiring the knowledge of self-transcendence.

Devote yourself to the Good, not only for your own good, but above all for the love of the Good itself.

The truly great individual is the one who realizes his or her own unimportance before the infinite life.

Do not deliberately impose yourself on others, for it drives away affinity; you cannot do without other's help in carrying out your task.

Never think that your own pain is worse than your neighbor's, or that the situations that please you should also please those who follow you. What encourages you may frighten others, and what makes you happy may be poison to others.

Above all, fight the tendency to be personally offended with the same persistence you use to keep your bed clean. Most offences are dead weights on our heart. Is not holding on to the insults and sarcasm by others not the same as growing someone else's thorns in our home?

Clear your mind each morning, and go forward in the certainty that we will settle our accounts with the One who has lent us life and not with those who have squandered it.

Let reality clarify your vision and you will find the divine happiness of the nameless angel who works for the common good.

Learn to be alone so that you can be freer in carrying out the duty that unites you to all others, and keep your mind on the Heavenly Friend, who took the narrow way of the cross. Let us not forget Paul's warning regarding material possessions when he says that, "We brought nothing into this world, and we can take nothing when we leave it."

~ 48 ~

In the Lord's Presence

> *"Why is my language not clear to you?*
> *Because you are unable to hear what I say."*
> Jesus. (Jn. 8:43)

Christ's language has always seemed incomprehensible and strange to many learners of the Gospel:

Doing as much good as possible, even when evils are numerous and on the increase.

Lending without expecting repayment.

Forgiving always.

Loving one's enemies.

Helping slanderers and other bad people.

Many people listen to the Good News but they cannot grasp its teachings.

This happens to so many followers of the Gospel because they use their mental energy in other areas.

They vaguely believe in heaven's help in times of suffering, but show a complete lack of interest in studying and applying the Divine Laws.

The worries connected with ownership envelop their existence.

They want the gold of the earth, the bread of the storehouse, usable linen, good health, the pleasures of the senses, and social respect so much that they do not remember that they are mere beneficiaries of the world. They never think about the temporariness of all material assets, whose sole function is to provide them with an appropriate environment for working in charity and in the light for the elevation of the eternal spirit.

They hear Christ's call, but their attention is riveted to the appeals of the physical life.

They hear, but they do not listen.

They are informed, but do not understand.

In this arena of contradictions, we always have respectable persons, and sometimes wonderful friends.

They hold immense potential of goodness in their hearts, but their minds are always occupied with perishable forms.

They are invaluable work stations, but their equipment is used for more or less pointless activities.

Therefore, let us not forget that it is always easy to hear the language of the Lord, but it is essential to present to him a heart free of residues of the earth in order to receive the divine word in spirit and in truth.

~ 49 ~

Fraternal Union

Seek to maintain the unity of the Spirit through the bond of peace. – Paul (Eph. 4:3)

Thousands of ways are shown to you every time you set your eyes on the distant goal ahead.

There are millions of pathways bordering yours.

Do not forget the road that is your own and go forward without fear.

You would probably like for all other roads to be subordinate to yours, and you see unity as being all travelers gravitating around your steps...

But join others without expecting them to join you.

Search for what is useful and beautiful, holy and sublime and press on...

The headspring seeks the stream; the stream seeks the river, and the river connects to the sea.

Let us not to forget that spiritual unity is the basic work of peace.

Do you see those who devote themselves to children?

Do you see friend who dedicate themselves to helping the sick?

Do you see the care of those who have made themselves friends of the elderly and the young?

Do you see the effort of those who have dedicated themselves to the improvement of the soil or to the training of animals?

Do you appreciate the work of those who preach to spread the Good?

Honor all of them with your gesture of sympathy and serenity, convinced that only the roots of understanding can uphold the tree of fraternal unity, which we all want to be robust and fruitful.

Do not think that the others see life the way you see it.

Evolution is an infinite stairway. Each one beholds the landscape according to the step on which he or she is standing.

Approach all workers of the Good and offer them the best you can, and they will answer with what is best of themselves.

War is always the poisonous fruit of violence.

The sterile argument is a result of imposition.

Fraternal unity is the sublime dream of the human soul; nevertheless, it will not be achieved unless we respect one another, cultivating harmony in the environment in which we were called to serve. It is only by "making every effort to maintain the unity of Spirit through the bond of peace" that we will achieve such realization.

~ 50 ~

Let Us Go Forward

Brothers, as for me, I do not consider myself as having already reached perfection. But one thing I do: I have forgotten the things I left behind and I go forward to those that lie ahead. – Paul. (Phil. 3:13, 14)

On the Christian pathway, we are always meeting large numbers of brothers and sisters who are lingering in the shadow of unproductivity, declaring themselves victims of spiritual setbacks.

It is someone who is weeping from having lost a loved one that was called to the transformation of the grave.

It is a worker who has been hurt by the misunderstanding of a friend.

It is the missionary who has stopped because of slander.

It is the one who regrets the desertion of a partner in the good cause.

It is the worker of the Good who complains endlessly about having been abandoned by his spouse because she could not understand his loving dedication.

It is the wife who is constantly grumbling about how much her family misunderstands her.

It is the idealist who waits for a material fortune to begin the work he or she has been called to do.

It is the person who is waiting for a well-paying job before devoting him or herself to good works.

It is the person who feels scandalized by other people's faults, thus freezing his or her ability to serve.

It is the person who deplores a wrong he or she committed, wasting the blessings of time on destructive remorse.

The past may be filled with the virtues of experience, but it is not always the best conductor of life for the future.

It is essential to guard the heart against all the numbing coverings that often enshroud our soul.

Contrition, longing, hope and scruples are sacred, but they should not constitute obstacles that keep our spirit from accessing the Higher Realms.

Paul of Tarsus, who had been familiar with the terrible aspects of human struggle deep within his own heart, reached the heights of Christ's apostolate, and he offers us the sure route to spiritual growth.

"Let us forget all the bad experiences of yesterday and let us go forward towards the days of enlightenment that await us," is the essence of his fraternal advice to the Philippians.

Let us focus our energies on Jesus and press on.

No one can progress without self-renewal.

~ 51 ~

Open Graves

Their throats are open graves. —
Paul. (Rom. 3:13)

When talking about spirits who have strayed from the light, Paul says that their throats are like open graves. We can use this image to define many individuals when they abandon the True Pathway of the Gospel for the scabrous trails of egotism.

They soon begin to reside in the dark empire of the "self," forgetting the obligations that place us in the Divine Kingdom of Universality, and their throats really do become veritable open graves. They emit all the poisonous gall that flows from within them, like a vase of muck, and they begin to attune themselves exclusively to the problems that trouble their neighbors, friends and loved ones.

They see only the faults, weak points and unwholesome aspects of the people of goodwill who share in their evolutionary progress.

They weave long commentaries in examining other people's ulcers, instead of curing them.

They waste precious time on long, inhumane conversations, belittling other people's intentions.

They overburden their imaginations with depressing images, in the realms of suspicion and mental intemperance.

All said, they complain about everything and everyone.

They send out numbing emanations of ill-will, spreading discouragement and distrust against the prosperity of sanctification wherever they go, wilting the flowers of hope and destroying the unripe fruits of charity.

Such learners, deeply unfortunate because of their conduct, do, in fact, resemble open graves…

They exhale the decay and poisons of death.

Therefore, when you leave the pathway for the slippery terrain of undue lamentations and accusations, reconsider your spiritual steps and remember that our throats should be devoted to the Good, for only then can the sublime words of the Lord be expressed through them.

~ 52 ~

Serving and Progressing

Therefore, lift up the tired hands and the weak knees. – Paul. (Heb. 12:12)

If in ordinary farming it is difficult to raise a wholesome crop so that the world's storehouses do not lack bread for the body, toiling to acquire the spiritual qualities that comprise the living and imperishable food for the soul is almost sacrificial.

The seed of goodwill has, in fact, been planted, but a thousand obstacles impair its germination and growth.

It is the silt of the futilities of the inferior life.

The invasion of worms represented by all kinds of annoyances.

The clay of envy and spite.

The thunder of miscomprehension.

The hail of evil.

The detritus of slander.

The heat wave of responsibility.

The cold-spell of indifference.

The draught of misunderstanding.

The crabgrass of ignorance.

The clouds of worry.

The dust of disillusionment.

It is as if all the imponderable forces of the human experience have come together against those who want to progress on the pathway of the Good.

While we have not yet reached the divine inheritance for which we are destined, any fall can easily happen…

The ascent is the toil of sweat, persistence and sacrifice.

If your heart is truly interested in the upper environs of life, do not retreat before the struggle.

Though faced with every sort of difficulty, go forward, offering to your endeavor of perfection all that is noble, beautiful and useful.

Remember Paul's advice and do not stand still.

Move your exhausted hands, raise your weak knees and get busy, being sure that in order to get the best out of life, you have to serve and evolve without stopping.

53

On Preaching

I will gladly spend everything I have for you, and I will even expend myself for you, as well, even if I love you more, while you love me less. – Paul. (2 Cor. 12:15)

There are many who preach salvation, who gladly ascend the golden pulpit to preach the merits of goodness and faith. However, when invited to contribute financially to good works, they feel wounded in their wallets, and they hurriedly leave, making silly excuses.

A thousands obstacles prevent them from practicing charity and they leave for other parts, where the good doctrine does not inconvenience their peaceful lives.

Actually, in the true practice of the Gospel we are not only to spend what we have but also to give something of ourselves.

It is not enough to open the coffer to solve problems related to the physical life.

It is essential to give of ourselves through the sweat of cooperation and through the willing effort of solidarity so that we may be able to fulfil our primary duties to Christ.

Those who do not make an effort on behalf of others only know the lessons of the Almighty in the circles of talk.

Many people first wait to receive love from others in order to love in return. Yet, such an attitude only means delaying the sanctifying undertakings that are our responsibility.

Those who help others and suffer for the Gospel receive a heavenly supply of strength to act for overall progress.

Let us remember that, on behalf of others, Jesus not only gave what he could have retained to his own benefit, but he donated of himself for the general evolution.

Preachers who do not want to spend or give of themselves for the spread of the redemptive ideas of Christianity are like orchids of the Gospel resting on the problematic support of others' potential. But those who teach and exemplify, learning to sacrifice themselves for everyone's spiritual growth, are like the robust tree of the Eternal Good, manifesting the Lord on the rich soil of true fraternity.

~ 54 ~

Let Us Seek Eagerly

But eagerly seek the better gifts. And now I will show you an even more excellent way. – Paul. (1 Cor. 12:31)

The idea that no one should strive to learn and better themselves in order to be more useful to the Divine Revelation is more of an attempt to encourage idleness than a show of incipient humility.

Life is an advanced course on improving oneself through effort and struggle. If the stone itself must go through the polishing process in order to reflect the light, then what about we, who have been called to exteriorize the divine resources?

None should stop the blessed work of their learning process under the pretext of collaborating with heaven, for progress is like a tireless convoy that leaves behind those who rebel against the need to continue progressing.

It is indispensable to keep up with the evolution of everything around us.

The Gospel does not endorse an attitude of careless expectation.

The words of Paul are extremely significant.

When speaking to the Corinthians, the Apostle to the Gentiles exhorts them to eagerly seek the better gifts.

It is essential that we be determined to acquire the best qualities of the heart and the mind to purify our imperishable individuality.

Learning and sanctification through toil and fraternity are everyone's duties.

Self-improvement is everyone's obligation.

Let us zealously work on our spiritual growth, marking our presence with the blessings of working on behalf of all wherever we go, and as soon as we become part of this worthy effort by means of personal and incessant dedication to the Good, heaven will show us more illuminated pathways for ascending higher.

~ 55 ~

Elucidations

For we do not preach ourselves, but Jesus Christ the Lord, and ourselves as your servants for Jesus' sake. – Paul. (2 Cor. 4:5)

When we are in real communion with the Lord, we disciples of the Good News cannot ignore the need to lessen our individuality so that we can more effectively disseminate the teachings of the Master to the multitude.

Regarding the Christian life, rightly considered, the only justifiable passions are those of learning, helping and serving, for we know that Christ is the Great Planner of our accomplishments.

If we remember that his watch-care is always for those who work for the Good, we will always be attentive to our duties, being sure that his teachings remain invariable in all the circumstances of life.

Therefore, wherever we are, our fundamental concern should be service rendered in his name, being aware that the preaching of ourselves by means of the peculiar particularisms of our personality is always the interference of our ego in the Kingdom of God's endeavors of the eternal life.

In writing to the Corinthians, Paul defines his own position and that of all the other apostles as being servants of the community out of love for Jesus. There cannot be a clearer definition of our responsibilities.

The Divine Master's leadership becomes clearer and clearer, and the general planning of the tasks reserved for disciples of all conditions is structured on his Gospel of Wisdom and Love.

Let us seek the foundations of Christ so that we may not act in vain.

Let us adjust ourselves to the consciousness of the Great Renewer so that we may not be tempted by our impulses of control, since in every circumstance and situation, the follower of the Good News is invited, called and constrained to serve.

~ 56 ~

Be Born again Now

"I tell you the truth: no one can see the Kingdom of God unless he is born again." — Jesus. (Jn. 3:3)

Nature holds valuable lessons in this respect. Years pass with mathematical precision; nevertheless, each day is a new day. Since people have three hundred and sixty five opportunities per year to learn and to start again, how many opportunities for moral renewal will there be in the blessed period of an entire lifetime?

Keep what is good and just, beautiful and worthy from the past, but do not hold on to the darkness and detritus, even when they are disguised in enchanting clothing.

In your endeavors of true fraternity, do your own share; do not shoulder your spirit benefactors and friends with it.

Each new hour may bring readjustment.

If possible, do not put off till later the ties of peace and love you can create now by replacing the heavy shackles of disaffection.

It is not easy to break our old preconceptions about the world, or open our hearts and forgive those who have hurt us. Nonetheless, the best antidote against the poison of aversion is our goodwill towards those that hate or misunderstand us.

While we are holed up in our defensive fortress, our adversary thinks of ways to come up with more ammunition against us. However, if we face the situation fearlessly and calmly, showing a new attitude in the conflict, the idea of peace replaces the dark fermentation of war inside and around us.

Has someone offended you? Exercise understanding once more.

Has someone misunderstood you? Persevere in demonstrating the best intentions.

Revitalize yourself each day in the crystal-clear and incessant stream of the Good.

Do not forget the Master's words: "No one can see the Kingdom of God unless he is born again."

Be born again right now regarding your objectives, resolutions and attitudes, working to overcome the obstacles around you and anticipating the victory over yourself in due time…

It is better to help today than to be helped tomorrow.

57

Apostles

For it seems to me that God has put us apostles last, like men condemned to death, for we have been made spectacles to the world, to angels and to men. — Paul. (1 Cor. 4:9)

An apostle is an educator par excellence. Willingness to work and self-sacrifice live within him or her so that the mind of his or her disciples may be transformed and illumined on their ascent toward higher spheres.

The legislator makes laws that lead to balance and justice in the social arena.

The administrator uses material and human resources to provide services.

The cleric teaches the layperson about the faith in its primary expressions.

The artist embellishes the way to the mind by opening the heart to the edifying messages that the world encompasses in its content of spirituality.

The scientist is in awe before the realities that the Divine Wisdom has created for human evolution and he or she reveals them to people in a clear and perceptible way.

The thinker asks questions, probing transitory phenomena.

The doctor aids the sick.

The soldier keeps the crowd in order.

The worker is the active minstrel of material forms, improving those meant for the preservation of life.

Apostles, however, are guides for the spirit.

In all the great causes of humankind, they are living institutions of the revealing example, living amid the world of causes and effects and showing in themselves the essence of what they teach, the truth they demonstrate, and the light they make shine around others. They influence the thoughts of the wise and the ignorant, the rich and the poor, the great and the humble, renewing their way of believing and being so that the world may be uplifted and sanctified. Within them arises the equation of facts and ideas, with which they make themselves pioneers or defenders by completely giving themselves to others. Hence, they toil and struggle, suffer and grow without rest, facing the many crosses of pain and incomprehension. They represent the spiritual yeast that leavens the loaf of progress and improvement. According to Paul of Tarsus, they move through this world like prisoners who are condemned to incessant suffering, as if Divine Providence has placed them in the worst position of the human experience. This is because within them we find the positive demonstration of the Good to the world, the possibility of being instruments of high order spirits and the source of imperishable benefits for all humankind.

~ 58 ~

Disciples

"And anyone who does not take up his cross and follow me cannot be my disciple."
Jesus. (Lk. 14:27)

The most varied Christian circles are replete with students who enthusiastically proclaim themselves to be disciples of Jesus, as if true devotion to the Master were a matter of mere words.

In reality, however, the Gospel leaves no room for doubt about the matter.

The life of each conscious person entails a set of duties towards him or herself, the family of souls that gather around his or her sentiments, and towards all humankind.

It is not so easy to fulfill all such duties in full accordance with the evangelical guidelines.

It is essential that we eliminate the rough edges of our temperament, ensuring our spiritual balance, that we contribute effectively on behalf of all those who share our pathway, giving to each one what belongs to him or her, and that we serve our community.

Unless we rectify ourselves, we cannot correct our pathway.

Twisted trees do not project perfect images.

If we are searching for sublimation in Christ, then we should heed the divine lessons. In order to be his disciples, we must firmly set out to take up the cross of our testimony of having assimilated the Good, following in his footsteps.

There are learners that do take up their crosses of redemptive trials, but they do not follow the Lord; rather, they give in to rebelliousness by hardening their hearts and running away.

There are others who follow the Master with well-made words and phrases, but they do not take up their cross, leaving it at the door of their neighbors and fellow believers.

Duty and renewal.

Work and self-improvement.

Action and progress.

Responsibility and spiritual growth.

Acceptance of the imperatives of the Good and obedience to the standards of the Lord.

Only after such achievements will we experience true communion with the Divine Master.

～ 59 ～

Words of Eternal Life

"You have the words of eternal life." –
Peter. (Jn. 6:68)

Words surround you in every phase of the struggle and in every aspect of the way.

Respectable words related to your duties.

Friendly words brought to you by devoted brothers and sisters, encouraging and consoling you.

Opinions about things that have nothing to do with you.

Suggestions of all sorts.

Invaluable lectures.

Empty conversations that your ears cast to the wind.

Spoken words ... written words...

Nonetheless, in these many spoken or silent verbal expressions, amidst which your mind develops, you will find the words of eternal life.

Keep your heart on the alert for them.

They come from the unfathomable love of Christ, like pure water from the immense bosom of the earth.

You are often distracted and do not heed their warning, their melody, their lesson or their beauty.

Remain heedful, isolated from yourself, so that you do not miss their flavor and light.

They exhort you to ponder the grandeur of God and to live in accordance with his Laws.

They refer to the planet as our home and to humankind as our family.

They show us that love is the bond that unites us to everyone else.

They point to toil as our pathway of evolution and spiritual growth.

They unveil the divine horizons of life and teach us to lift up our eyes higher and farther.

"Words, words, words…"

Forget those that incite you to uselessness and employ all that indicate your just duties and teach you to make life greater; but do not neglect words that awaken you to the light and the Good. They can enter our heart through a friend, a letter, a page or a book, but in essence, they always come from Jesus, the Divine Friend of us all.

Keep the words of eternal life with you, for they are sanctifiers of the spirit in daily life, and, most of all, our sure mental support in the difficult times of great renewal.

~ 60 ~

Alms

"But give what you have to the poor." — Jesus. (Lk. 11:41)

The word of the Lord is always based on a luminous beauty that we must not lose sight of.

Regarding alms, the Master's recommendation in this verse from Luke deserves special attention.

"But give what you have to the poor."

Giving what we have is different than giving from what we keep.

Charity is sublime in every aspect. Under no circumstances should we forget the wonderful selflessness of those who distribute bread and clothing, medicine and assistance for the body, learning solidarity and teaching it.

However, we must point out the fact that wealth and authority are temporary possessions that we keep on our journey, and that in the essential foundations of life, they do not belong to us.

The Owner of all the power and wealth in the universe is God, our Creator and Father, who lends them to men and women, according to their merits or necessities.

Consequently, let us not neglect the *alms* of our inner world, and let us ask ourselves:

What do we have of ourselves to give?

What kind of emotion are we communicating to others?

What reactions are we provoking from our neighbor?

What are we giving to our brothers and sisters of the daily struggle?

What is the stockpile of our sentiments?

What kind of vibrations are we emitting?

In order to disseminate goodness, no one has to laugh loudly or smile unnaturally. Instead, in order to avoid offering stones of indifference to hearts starving for the bread of fraternity, we must develop in our spirit the reserves of understanding, spreading the treasure of friendship and empathy that the Master has entrusted to us in working for the good of all those around us, whether they are near or far away.

The charity that fills the stomach but that never forgets an offense, that never serves personally, or that does not light a torch to banish ignorance is always limited.

The Divine Instructor's recommendation in this verse from Luke means: give alms from your inner life; assist personally; spread joy and courage, opportunity for growth and edification amongst others; and be dedicated brothers and sisters to your neighbors, for in truth, love that is given amid blessings of happiness and work, peace and trust, is always the best gift of all.

~ 61 ~

Never Give Up

... always pray and never give up. –
(Lk. 18:1)

Do not let external problems, including those involving your own body, render you incapable of working on your self-illumination.

As long as you are living on a plane of practice such as the earth, you will continue to be confronted with problems and suffering.

A lesson learned is something that leads to more lessons.

Behind a mystery solved lie other mysteries.

The purpose of a school is none other than teaching, practicing and improving.

Thus, be filled with enthusiasm and goodwill in every situation.

You were placed amidst a thousand strange obstacles so that by overcoming outer difficulties, you may learn to surpass your inner limitations.

As long as humankind has not adapted to the New Light, you will live surrounded by troubling tears, thoughtless attitudes and bad sentiments.

Always be willing to forgive and help, so that you do not miss a glorious opportunity for spiritual growth.

Remember all the afflictions that have beset the Christian spirit in the world ever since the Lord's coming.

What has become of the Sanhedrin that condemned the Heavenly Friend to death?

What has become of the proud, domineering Romans?

Where are the persecutors of the nascent Gospel?

Where are the soldiers who caused dark rivers of blood and sweat to flow around the Gospel?

What has become of the shrewd rulers that fought and did business in the name of the Crucified Renewer?

Where is the darkness of the Middle Ages?

Where are the politicians and inquisitors of every sort, who tortured in the name of the Magnificent Benefactor?

Swept away by time over the cliffs of ash, they strengthened and solidified the pedestal of light on which the image of Christ shines ever more glorious in the governance of the centuries.

Focus on the endeavor of helping for the common good, bearing your cross on the road to divine resurrection. When caught off guard by unpleasant surprises along the way, remember that, before anything else, the most important thing is to pray always, toiling, serving, learning, loving and never giving up.

~ 62 ~

Slowly but Surely

Our outer man may be wasting away, but our inner man is being renewed day by day. –
Paul. (2 Cor. 4:16)

Observe the line of sequence and gradation that prevails in the smallest areas of nature.

Nothing happens all at once, and there is no privilege anywhere on the stage of the Divine Law.

The ear is filled with corn kernel by kernel.

The tree grows millimeter by millimeter.

The forest begins with insignificant seeds.

The edifice is raised brick by brick.

The piece of cloth is woven thread by thread.

The most famous pages were written letter by letter.

The wealthiest city is built inch by inch.

The greatest fortunes of gold and precious stones were extracted from the soil piece by piece.

The longest highway is paved meter by meter.

The great river that empties into the sea is a coming together of many streams.

Do not give up on your wonderful dream of knowledge and accomplishment in the higher realms of the mind and sentiments, but remember your small daily tasks.

Everywhere, life is a process of renewal, and according to Paul's sublime words, even as the flesh wastes away, the imperishable individuality is incessantly renewed.

Nonetheless, so that we may not change ourselves in the opposite direction to the one expected by the Most High, it is essential that we constantly watch ourselves and persevere in our efforts of self-improvement in the activity that helps and ennobles us.

If some divine ideal inhabits your mind, do not forget your small daily chores so that it may become a reality when the time is right.

Is there a favorable occasion for its accomplishment?

Then act sensibly with your soul focused on your goal.

Are there troubles and struggles, thorns and stones on your pathway?

Press on, even so.

Time, that implacable dominator of civilizations and humankind, marches on at the rate of only sixty minutes per hour, but it never stops.

Let us remember the lesson and go forward with the best that we are.

Slowly, but surely.

63

Differences

"By this all will know that you are my disciples: if you love one another." — Jesus. (Jn. 13:35)

In the many denominations of Christianity, there are thousands of people who are attached to their Master and Lord in some manner.

There are hearts that outdo themselves in their praise for the Great Physician, exalting him for his divine intercession in matters in which they realize they were benefited, but they do not go beyond making spectacular claims, as if they were living forever immersed in wonderful visions.

They are simply beneficiaries and dreamers.

There are ardent temperaments that speak impressively from the pulpit when giving erudite and emotion-packed sermons, in which they expound the role of the Great Renewer in religion, philosophy and history. Yet, they do not go beyond these invaluable speeches.

They are priests and preachers – nothing more.

There are brilliant minds that pour forth sublime pages of consoling faith, causing tears of emotion to flow from readers avid for revelatory knowledge. Even so, they do not go beyond the arena of religious erudition.

They are but writers and intellectuals.

These all have their special abilities and merits.

On the other hand, there is a different kind of collaborator regarding the work of the Good News.

Such individuals praise the Lord with their thoughts, words and actions every day.

Yes, they do spread the treasure of the Good through consoling words whenever possible.

They do pen edifying concepts about the Gospel every time the circumstances allow it.

However, they go beyond spoken or written sermons. The act incessantly in the sowing of the Good by means of deeds of self-sacrifice and pure love, according to the examples of action that Christ bequeathed to us. They do not ask for compensation or results, nor are they in tune with evil. They always help and bless.

Such persons are recognized as true disciples of the Master by loving much.

~ 64 ~

Sowers

"A sower went out to sow his seed." — Jesus. (Mt. 13:3)

Every one of the Divine Master's lessons is profound and sublime down to the smallest detail. When he begins narrating the parable of the sower, he starts with a lesson of inestimable importance worth remembering.

He does not say that the sower has a contract with third parties, but that he himself went out to sow.

Transferring this image to the soil of the spirit, in which so many imperatives of renewal invite workers of goodwill to the sanctifying farming of spiritual growth, we are led to realize that servants of the Gospel are compelled to go out personally in order to benefit others' hearts.

It is necessary to tear down the old prison of the "point of view" and devote ourselves to serving our neighbor.

As we learn the science of extracting ourselves from the dark jail of the "self," we start a journey through the great continent called "everyone's interest." And in its infinite expanse, we find the "land of the souls" choked with thorns, filled with misery, covered with stones or poisoned with mire, thus offering us a divine opportunity to act for the good of all.

It was according to this script that the Divine Sower staged his ministry of light, starting his heavenly mission of assistance amidst humble shepherds, then continuing it amongst the friends of Nazareth and the scholars of Jerusalem, amongst verbose Pharisees and simple fishermen, the righteous and the unrighteous, the rich and the poor, the sick in body and soul, the old and the young, women and children…

As we have said, the Sower from Heaven left his grandeur and came to us to spread the light of Revelation and to increase our vision and discernment. And even though he could have been replaced by thousands of messengers if he had wanted to, he humbled himself so that we could be exalted, and he put himself in darkness so that our light might shine.

Therefore, let us leave our inhibitions behind and learn with the Master to "go out to sow."

~ 65 ~

Be Not Deceived

Are you looking at things only according to appearances? If anyone is confident that he belongs to Christ, he should remember that we belong to Christ as much as he does. — Paul. (2 Cor. 10:7)

Do not be deceived about our common need of self-improvement.

Many times, by overestimating our true worth, we see ourselves as privileged people in the art of spiritual growth. In such circumstances, we often thoughtlessly forget that others are doing much more for the Good than we are.

The firefly gives off tiny flashes in the darkness and imagines itself to be the prince of light, but then it discovers the candle flame that drowns it out. The candle flame sits proudly atop a mantel and believes it is on the absolute throne of light; however, there comes a day when the electric lamp shines from the ceiling and obscures its flame. The lamp in turn becomes haughty on the public square, but each morning the sun shines in the sky, illuminating the entire earth and paling both large and small planetary lights.

As long as the protecting and educating darkness of the flesh remains, we are frequently the victims of our own illusions, but as the infinite brightness of the truth returns with the renewal of physical death, we can see in the sun of the spirit world that Divine Providence is glorious love for all humankind.

Do not exchange reality for appearances.

Let us respect each accomplishment in its time and each person in his or her due place.

We are all brothers and sisters on the pathway of evolution and spiritual growth, although we are still caught between good and evil. Wherever we activate our "inferior part," the shadow of others will be our company. From the point where we project our "good part," the light of our neighbor will come to meet us.

Each soul is an unknown to another soul. In light of this, it is not right to set the walls of our tranquility on the foundation of other people's sentiments.

Let us not be deceived.

Let us correct whatever may be harming our inner peace, and let us extend our fraternal arms and thoughts in every direction, being sure that if we have faults and virtues, when judgment time arrives we will always receive in accordance with our deeds. And by understanding that the goodness of the Lord shines on all without distinction of person, let us remember for our own and other people's sake Paul's meaningful words: "If anyone is confident that he belongs to Christ, he should remember that we belong to Christ as much as he does."

~ 66 ~

Wake Up and Rise

Wake up, you who sleep; rise from amongst the dead, and Christ will shine on you. — Paul. (Eph. 5:14)

Thousands of our brothers and sisters have been asleep with no sign of ever waking up while the glorious time of their life on earth passes uselessly by.

They vaguely perceive the ongoing production of nature, but they do not remember their obligation to do something for the progress of society.

Faced with the tree loading itself with fruit or the bee making its honeycomb, they do not remember the simple duty of contributing to the common prosperity.

Generally speaking, they resemble corpses decorated with costly adornments.

There comes a day, however, when they wake up and begin to praise the Lord in astonishing ecstasy…

But that is not enough.

There are many brothers and sisters whose eyes are open, yet their soul is in the horizontal position of idleness. Hearts that have awakened must arise to life, to the work of sowing and harvesting the Good so that the Master may shine on them.

Let us strive to alert our sleeping brothers and sisters, but let us not forget the need to help them emerge from that state of affairs.

We need to know how to mobilize the right means to aid those we are close to and those we are not close to, but who need to arise to the blessings of Jesus.

Making suggestions is not enough.

Those who prescribe service and virtue to their neighbor, without having first prepared their understanding by means of the spirit of fraternity, are like the strict instructor that demands from his or her students full knowledge of a certain book without having first taught them to read.

Paul said: "Wake up, you who sleep! Rise from among the dead, and Christ will shine on you." And we repeat: "Let us awaken to the superior life and arise in doing good works, and the Lord will help us so that we may help others."

~ 67 ~

Inner Renewal

Be renewed in the spirit of your minds. –
Paul. (Eph. 4:23)

Human beings have used reasoning for many centuries, heeding rules that are practically unchanging, and comparing external events according to old processes of observation. They run their physical lives, making great transformations in the area of fundamental organic procedures, and they use speech like someone using the elements that are indispensable for building a construction of stone, sand and lime.

Within the arena of exterior nature per se, modifications in any aspect of it have been minimal, except for the great progress made related to the techniques of science and industry.

In the arena of the sentiments, however, the changes have been profound.

Amongst highly educated peoples, no one tolerates the slavery of their fellow beings; no one plays with another's life with impunity, and no one applauds systematic and deliberate cruelty as they used to.

Through the heart, the ideal of humanity has been purifying the mind in all climes of the planet.

The home and the school, the place of worship and the hospital, the institutions of social security and charity are creations of sensibility, and not of calculation.

Workers may display lofty qualities of intelligence and skill, but if they are not devoted to their work, they will continue to be merely conscious, repetitive pieces of equipment, just as the stomach has been a machine of digestion for millennia.

Only through inner renewal does the soul progress on the road to a perfect life.

Before Christ, thousands of men and women died on crosses; however, the Master's cross became an inextinguishable light due to the quality of sentiment with which the Crucified One handed himself over to death, thus influencing the quality of sentiment of nations and centuries.

Growing in goodness and understanding means extending the vision and sanctifying the objectives of society.

Jesus came to us to teach us that Love, more than anything else, is the way to the Abundant Life.

Have you lived amidst pain, affliction, darkness or infirmity? Then renew your sentiments in accordance with the standards of the Gospel, and you will see the Divine Purpose of Life acting everywhere with justice and mercy, wisdom and understanding.

~ 68 ~

Sowing and Construction

For we are co-workers with God; you are God's field, God's building. – Paul. (1 Cor. 3:9)

By affirming his status as a co-worker of God and describing the Lord's followers and beneficiaries of the Gospel as the Lord's field and building, Paul painted the spiritual picture that will always exist on the evolving earth amongst those who already know the divine truth and those who do not know it.

If we have received the lighted torch of the Gospel for our journey, then we are automatically considered to be co-workers of Jesus' ministry. We are responsible for the sowing and construction of it amongst all those who share the pathway with us.

Thus, in essence we know what service the Revelation has in store for us as soon as we approach the Christian light.

If we have the Master's blessing in our heart, we are to restore balance to the currents of life wherever we are, helping those who cannot help themselves, seeing for those who cannot see, and hearing for those who cannot hear, so that the work of the Divine Kingdom may grow, progress and sanctify all the earth.

The work entails sowing and building, which demands everybody's personal effort and goodwill, for according to the apostle's symbolism, a plant needs time and care to grow, and a solid house cannot be built in one day.

Wherever we go, however, we see masons who complain about the weight of the brick and sand, and farmers who gripe about having to fertilize and protect the fragile plant.

Nevertheless, the lesson of the Gospel leaves no room for doubt.

If you already know Jesus' benefits, then you are one of his co-workers in the vineyard of the world and in the construction of the human spirit for the Eternal Life.

Press on in the endeavor that was entrusted to you and fear not. If faith is our crown of light, then working for others is our daily blessing.

~ 69 ~

Firmness and Perseverance

> *Therefore, my dear brothers, be firm and constant, always abundant in the Lord's work, knowing that your toil is not in vain.* – Paul (1 Cor. 15:58)

Many people believe that embracing the faith entitles them to unproductive ecstasy. Under the pretext of ensuring the illumination of their soul, many hearts flee the daily struggle, locking themselves up in the sanctuary of the home amidst vigils of worship and profound thinking about the divine mysteries. They forget that the whole of life is God's Universal Creation.

Faith means vision.

Vision means understanding and the ability to help.

Those who have entered the "Spiritual Land of Truth" have found in work a great blessing.

Neither the Lord nor his disciples lived only in contemplation.

Yes, they did pray, for no one can live without the inner shower of silence to renew their strength in the superior currents of sublime energy coming from the Heavenly Fountainhead.

Prayer and reflection are the subtle lubricant in our machine of daily experiences.

It is important to realize, however, that the Lord and his disciples struggled, served and suffered in the active cultivation of the Good, and that the Gospel entails constant toil for all those who adopt its principles of salvation.

Accepting Christianity means renewing oneself for the Higher Realms, and only the environment of service can restructure the spirit and sanctify its destiny.

Invariably peremptory in his warnings and admonishments, Paul of Tarsus, writing to the Corinthians, pointed out the need for our firmness and constancy in the endeavor of spiritual evolution so that we may be abundant in worthy actions for the Lord.

Helping others, creating joy, harmony and hope, opening new horizons to a higher kind of knowledge, and making life better wherever we are, comprises the ministry of all those who have devoted themselves to the Good News.

Let us seek the pure waters of prayer to soothe our hearts, but let us not forget to use our emotions, reasoning, and hands for the progress and improvement of ourselves, of everyone and everything, knowing that Jesus needs industrious workers to build his Kingdom on the entire earth.

~ 70 ~

Loneliness

Pilate asked them, "But what wrong has he done?" They shouted even louder, "Crucify him!" (Mt. 27:23)

As you evolve higher and higher by performing your duty, you experience the loneliness of the heights and immeasurable sadness afflicts your sensitive soul.

Where are those who used to laugh with you in the springtime park of your early youth? Where are the hearts that used to come looking for you in times of wonder? Where are those who used to partake of the bread and the dream with you in the cheerful adventures of the beginning?

Of course, they stayed behind...

They stayed in the valley, flying in a narrow circle like golden moths that go up in smoke at first contact with the smallest flame that appears before them.

There is light all around you, but also silence...

Within you, the happiness of knowing, but also the pain of not being understood...

Your voice cries out without an echo and your longing is in vain.

Nonetheless, if you really are evolving to a higher level, what ears can hear you from such a great distance, and what heart in need of comfort would readily grasp your lofty ideals?

You weep, ask and suffer...

However, what kind of rebirth is not painful?

In order to free itself, the bird destroys the cradle of bark in which it matured, and the seed must undergo decay in the ground in order to produce.

Loneliness in serving others creates greatness.

The bedrock that upholds the plain does so by itself, and the sun that nourishes the whole world shines alone.

Do not weary of learning the science of spiritual growth.

Remember the Lord, who mounted Calvary with the cross on his wounded shoulders. No one was with him during his gruesome death, except for two thieves being rightly punished for their crimes.

Remember him and press on...

Do not count the good deeds that you have done for others.

Trust in the Infinite Good that awaits you.

Do not wait for others on your journey of sacrifice and spiritual evolution. And do not forget that, for his ministry of redemption for all humankind, the Divine Friend not only lived, struggled and suffered alone, but was also persecuted and crucified.

~ 71 ~

Take the Opportunity

If anyone says, "I love God," yet hates his brother, he is a liar. For how can anyone who does not love his brother, whom he can see, love God, whom he cannot see?" (1 Jn. 4:20)

Life is a process of the soul's growth towards the Divine Grandeur.

Make the best of the struggles and problems along the way in order to grow, widening your circle of relationships and action.

Let us learn in order to teach.

Let us accumulate in order to help.

Let us become greater in order to protect.

Let us become educated in order to serve.

By doing and giving something, the soul is always going further...

By keeping a blessing to itself, the spirit often only adorns itself; but if it spreads its wealth around, it grows constantly.

By serving others, it is incorporated into the chorus of the joy it causes.

By teaching the student, it enjoys the benefits of the lesson.

By being of service, it progresses and sanctifies itself in the beauty of individual and collective experience.

By spreading healthy and lofty thoughts, it becomes a living fountain of blessing and happiness for everyone.

By willingly helping in the ministry of the Good, it enjoys the overall prosperity.

Therefore, give of yourself, of your strengths and resources, working constantly to implement new values, helping others for your own good.

The world is a long, long road of evolution and growth, where ignorance and weakness travel along with you.

Take this glorious opportunity for evolution that the physical sphere has conferred on you, and help those who come your way, without thinking about any payment.

Our neighbor is our point of contact with God.

If you are seeking the Father, then help your brother and sister; assist one another reciprocally because, in the enlightening words of the evangelist, "If anyone says, 'I love God,' yet hates his brother, he is a liar. For how can anyone who does not love his brother, whom he can see, love God, whom he cannot see?"

72

Incomprehension

I have made myself weak to the weak in order to win the weak. I have become all things to all men so that by any means possible I might save some. — Paul. (1 Cor. 9:22)

Inarguably, incomprehension is like darkness in the presence of light. However, if the call of the light resounds within your soul, go forward and fight the darkness in the smallest recesses of your pathway.

Nevertheless, do not forget the law of assistance, and keep its principles in mind before acting.

To lower oneself in order to help others is the divine art of those who have conscientiously reached for a loftier life.

The glaring light causes blindness.

If the stars of love and wisdom shine in your heart, do not humiliate those who are still lost in the fog of ignorance and evil.

Gradate your manifestations so that your assistance does not become destructive.

If the rain were to continuously flood the desert under the pretext of quenching its thirst, and if the sun were to mercilessly beat down on the lake to dry its moist clay, we would never have a climate suitable for life's needs.

Do not make yourself too superior to those beneath you, or too strong to those who are weak.

Not all the students of a school graduate all at once; just a few do each year.

Every privilege demands not only responsibility but also a sense of proportion.

Keep the constructive energy of the respectable example, but do not forget that the skill of teaching can only be completely successful if the teacher knows how to support, wait and repeat.

Therefore, do not complain about incomprehension by using uneasiness and disenchantment, harshness and bitterness.

On an endeavor of salvation and rectification, there is heavenly merit for those who descend into the swamp without becoming contaminated.

A ball of matter gets covered with mud when thrown into the muddy pit. Nevertheless, the ray of light shines within the abyss and then returns unchanged.

What would have become of us if Jesus had not dimmed his own brightness to make himself weak like us so that we could witness his redemptive mission? Like him, let us learn to lower ourselves, helping others without causing damage to ourselves.

To do so, we cannot forget the expressive statement of Paul of Tarsus when he affirms that, for the victory of the good, he made himself weak to the weak, and by any means possible, he became everything to everyone in order to uplift a few.

73

Fraternal Encouragement

And according to his riches in glory, my God will meet all your needs through Christ Jesus.
– Paul. (Phil. 4:19)

Do not think you are alone in the purifying struggle, for the Lord will meet all our needs.

Look up to the Almighty, but from time to time look behind you.

If you are in a position to serve, then do so and then press on.

Remember your brothers and sisters who live in indigence, without any resources.

Think about the mothers and fathers who must listen to their children crying with no means of drying their tears.

Observe the sick whose circumstances have taken them from their homes.

Stop for a moment and give a friendly look to a homeless child.

Contemplate the anguish of those who are mentally unbalanced, confused in the eclipse of reason.

Think of the physically disabled, shackled to dolorous immobility.

Think about the maternal hearts tormented by the disharmony and lack of bread in their home.

From time to time, stop your hurried pace in order to help the blind who walk in darkness.

Then, you might find that your own suffering vanishes before your very eyes.

If you have arms to help and a mind capable of reflecting on the good of your fellow beings, then you are truly better than a king who may possess a world of gold but is afraid to help another person.

When you manage to overcome your afflictions in order to create joy for others, then other people's happiness will seek you out wherever you may be to bring you happiness of your own.

May infirmity and sadness never impede your journey.

It is better for death to take us while we are hard at work than for us to wait for it in an easy chair.

My brothers and sisters, light a new flame of encouragement in your soul, and press on ... Be an angel of fraternity to those who follow you dominated by affliction, ignorance and suffering.

When you plant the joy of living in the hearts around you, then very soon the flowers and fruit of your sowing will enrich your pathway.

74

When there is Light

Christ's love constrains us. –
Paul (2 Cor. 5:14)

When Jesus finds sanctuary in people's hearts, the road they are on changes completely.

There is no longer any room for idle worship or faith without works.

Something undefinable in earthly language transforms their spirit.

Society regards them as being maladjusted; however, when disciples of the Gospel reach that point it seems to them that the Divine Worker has taken over the depths of their being.

All their views about life are renewed.

The pleasures of yesterday have become the broken idols of today.

The goals they used to pursue are now wrong pathways that have to be put aside.

They become persons that are easy to satisfy but very difficult to please.

The Master's voice, persuasive and gentle, exhorts them to serve without ceasing.

Their soul becomes a marvelous estuary, where their neighbors' sufferings are met; consequently, they endure the constant pressure of other people's pain.

Their physical life seems like a crucifix on which the Master suffers. Their body is a living cross on which the Lord writhes, crucified.

Their sole place of rest is their persevering toil for the general good.

They are dissatisfied, albeit resigned; firm in their faith, although anguished; they serve all, but are alone; they are impelled down the road by hidden and inexplicable urges.

These are the disciples that Paul describes as being constrained by the love of Christ. The heavenly light burns within them until they abandon the lower zones forever.

The world sees them as unsuitable and crazy.

Jesus sees them as vessels of blessings.

The blossom is a beautiful promise wherever it may be.

The ripened fruit, however, is sustenance for today.

Happy are those who spread hope, but blessed are the followers of Christ who sweat and suffer every day so that their brothers and sisters may find comfort and nourishment in the Lord!

~ 75 ~

Management

"Give an account of your management." – Jesus. (Lk. 16:2)

In essence, each person is a servant because of his or her endeavor in the work of the Supreme Father, and at the same time a manager because he or she is the holder of enormous potential in the sphere in which he or she toils.

A steward of the world is not only the one who becomes grey-headed in working for the common good in public or private companies, combating a thousand intrigues in order to fulfill his or her duty.

Each intelligence on earth will have to account for the resources that have been entrusted to it.

Wealth and authority are not the only values for which we will have to give an account today and tomorrow.

The physical body is a sacred temple.

Physical health is a treasure.

The opportunity to work is a blessing.

The chance to serve is a divine bequeathal.

The opportunity to learn is a door to freedom.

Time is an inestimable patrimony.

The home is a gift from heaven.

A friend is a benefactor.

A beneficial experience is a great achievement.

The opportunity to live in harmony with the Lord, our fellow beings and nature is a glory common to all.

Time devoted to helping those less blessed with resources or understanding is precious.

Ground to sow, ignorance to be enlightened and pain to be consoled are appeals that heaven wordlessly sends to the whole world.

So, what have you been doing with the invaluable talents that lie within your heart, in your hands and on your pathway? Look after your own endeavor for the Good before the Eternal One because a time will come when the Divine Power will say to you: "Give an account of your management."

~ 76 ~

Spiritual Yeast

Dot you not know that a little yeast leavens the entire lump? – Paul. (1 Cor. 5:6)

Yeast is a substance that excites other substances. Our life is always spiritual yeast, with which we influence other people's lives.

Nobody lives alone.

We are influenced by thousands of expressions from other people's thoughts, and thousands of other people are unavoidably influenced by ours.

The waves of our influence become attuned to the emissions of all those who know us directly or indirectly, and they weigh in the balance of the world for either good or evil.

Our words elicit words from those who listen to us, and any time we are not sincere, the person with whom we are conversing is probably not being sincere either.

Our manners and habits generate manners and habits of the same nature around us, especially in those who are beneath us in knowledge and experience.

Our attitudes and actions create attitudes and actions of the same level amongst those around us, for what we do touches the realm of other people's observation, thereby interfering with the development of their mental forces.

Consequently, the only procedure for renewing oneself spiritually is by accepting the suggestions of the Good and practicing them intensively in what we do.

However, in the origins of our determinations lies the idea.

The mind is therefore the seat of how we act personally, wherever we are.

Thought is spiritual yeast. First of all, it establishes attitudes; second, it creates habits; next it governs expressions and words, through which the individuality influences life and the world. Thus, if it has been regenerated, a person's thought will be straight and clean on the pathway that leads to the Lord.

77

Our Father

"Our Father..." – Jesus (Mt. 6:9)

The grandeur of the Lord's Prayer will never be properly understood by those of us who receive its divine lessons.

Its every word has the brightness of sublime light.

By the way that it begins, the Divine Master set its foundations on God, teaching that the Supreme Giver of Life should be for all of us the beginning and the end of our endeavors.

It is necessary to start and to continue in God, conforming our impulses to the divine plan, so that our work is not wasted on ruinous or useless activity.

The Universal Spirit of the Father will guide our humblest efforts, our thinking, speaking, teaching and doing.

Then, with a simple possessive pronoun, the Master extols the community.

After God, humankind is to be the fundamental theme of our lives

Either we will understand the need, afflictions, problems and struggles of all those around us, or we will be isolated in self-centeredness.

All the triumphs and failures that illuminate or darken the earth are somehow our own.

The tears of one hemisphere echo in the other.

The suffering of our neighbor is a warning for our own home.

If we thoroughly examine the mistake of a brother or sister, we find that it is our mistake too, for we are imperfect components of an imperfect society, generating dangerous causes, and that is why the tragedies and failures of others affect us inside.

When we understand such reality, the "empire of the self" will be transformed into a blessed cell of the sanctifying life.

Without love for God and humankind, we are not sufficiently secure in this prayer.

"Our Father"… said Jesus to begin it.

Father of the Universe … Our world…

Unless we associate ourselves with the purposes of the Father in the small task we were allowed to do, our prayer will often be a simple repetition of "I want this or that," a prayer invariably full of desires, but almost always empty of sensibleness and love.

~ 78 ~

Divine Grafting

And if they do not persist in unbelief, they will be grafted in, for God is able to graft them in again. – Paul. (Rom. 11:23.)

Every human being is actually a spiritual plant, an object of great care on the part of the Divine Sower.

Each person, like the plant, has different phases of existence.

Sowing, germination, fertilization, growth, usefulness, blooming, fructification, harvest…

Shortly before the fruit appears, the fruit-grower is more carefully devoted to the tree.

Abundance and usefulness are crucial.

Likewise, the Lord adopts the same rules for us in the spiritual struggle.

As we acquire knowledge, reason and experience, the Heavenly Fruit-Grower confers on us invaluable resources of spiritual grafting with a view to our purification for life eternal.

On each new day of your human experience, you receive invaluable resources so that the results of your current incarnation may enrich you with divine light by means of the happiness you transmit to others. However, you are a "conscious tree," and are free to accept or not accept renewing elements, and you are free to acknowledge their blessing or reject it.

Carefully reflect on how many times the Sublime Sower has called you to grow spiritually.

Heaven's grafting-in searches for us in a thousand ways.

Today, it may be found in an edifying conversation.

Tomorrow, it may be found in an instructive book.

The day after that, it may be found in an apparently insignificant gift that comes your way.

So, if you intend to grow spiritually, take advantage of heaven's contributions, illuminating and sanctifying your inner temple. But if disbelief is currently isolating your mind, winding your energies around the reel of selfishness, the grafting-in of sublimation will search for you in vain, since in the area of the spirit, you still do not produce the sap that favors the Abundant Life.

79

Let Us Follow Peace

Seek peace and follow it. – Peter (1 Pet. 3:11)

Many people search for peace; very few try to follow it.

There are those who desire tranquility by any means; they sigh for it and seek it in many places. However, they lose it as soon as the Lord gives them what they asked for.

For instance, some people ask for material fortune, thinking it will bring them peace. Nevertheless, with the appearance of abundant wealth, they are tormented by a thousand problems because they do not know how to distribute, help, manage or spend it with simplicity.

Other people pray for the blessing of marriage, but when the Father grants it, they do not know how to be fraternal toward their spouse but are exasperated by all sorts of annoyances

Still others request special positions of trust in areas of public usefulness, but when they find themselves honored with popularity and the expectations of many people, they abandon the blessings of their work and flee in fright.

Peace is not physical indolence. It is health and spiritual joy.

If it is true that all search for peace in their own way, it is crucial to realize that true peace is the result of a balance between our own wishes and the purposes of the Lord in whatever position we may find ourselves.

Once we have received the task that heaven has entrusted to us, we have to know how to use the opportunity for our evolution and spiritual growth.

Peter said: "Seek peace and follow it."

However, in whatever situation we may find ourselves, there is no real peace without Christ within us; and the formula for integrating our souls with Jesus is invariable: "Let him deny himself, take up his cross and follow me." Unless we as human learners adapt our efforts to the renewing impulse of the Divine Master, instead of peace we will continue to have an ongoing war inside our hearts.

~ 80 ~

Fattened Hearts

You have fattened your hearts as on a day of a slaughter. (James 5:5)

The sun – that supreme expression of the Vital Divinity in the terrestrial firmament – works for the prosperity and perfection of the world.

The worm in the ground works to make the soil suitable for seeds.

The breeze makes its contribution by carrying pollen from flower to flower.

The water toils incessantly to enrich and purify physical life.

The tree provides blossoms, bears fruit, and regenerates the atmosphere.

The animal cooperates with humans and helps them with their accomplishments, sweating and dying so that beings of superior intelligence can enjoy a normal life.

The unbreakable law of labor governs the universe.

In the constancy of its benefits, movement and order are its essential characteristics.

Nevertheless, there are millions of people who feel themselves exonerated from the glory of serving.

For such persons, in whose brains reason sleeps, dull and empty, labor means degradation, humiliation, hell and suffering. They pursue a life of criminal imprudence with the same instinct as a fly in search of garbage. Once they find it, they use their time and potential for uncontrolled self-centeredness, like a well with stagnant water that is easily poisoned.

In fact, according to the fortunate expression of the apostle, they are "fattened hearts." They spin thick webs of hatred and selfishness, indifference and vanity, pride and indolence around themselves, and spiral down, out of control, through the heavy vibrations in which they are enveloped, towards a lower level of life, where, of course, many are waiting to take advantage of them, like persons fattening animals for the slaughter.

~ 81 ~

The Living Lamp

"Nor do people light a lamp and then put it under a bushel; they put it on a lampstand so that it may shine light on everyone in the house." — Jesus. (Mt. 5:15)

Many believers interpret such words as these of the Master as an appeal to regular preaching, and consequently deliver vehement sermons. Others believe that the Lord has imposed on them the obligation to violate their neighbor through a compulsory dissemination of the faith according to their own particular point of view.

In fact, edifying sermons and fraternal assistance are indeed indispensable for spreading the divine benefits of faith.

Without the word, the diffusion of knowledge is almost impossible. Without neighborly assistance, fraternity will never become a reality in this world.

This assertion by Jesus goes even further, however.

Let us reflect on the symbol of the lamp. It consumes power or fuel in order to give off light.

Without the sacrifice of energy or oil there is no light.

For us, here, the material for our maintenance is potential, resource, life.

Our existence is a living lamp.

It is a lamentable mistake to waste our energies without benefiting anyone, using them for our selfishness, vanity or personal limitation.

Let us put our potential at the disposal of our neighbor.

No one should keep the advantages of the earthly experience solely to him or herself. Each spirit temporarily incarnated in the human sphere enjoys broad prerogatives regarding spreading the Good, if he or she perseveres in the practice of Universal Love.

Therefore, preach the revelations of the Almighty, making them lovelier and more brilliant on your lips; talk to your relatives and friends so that they may accept the imperishable truths; but do not forget that the living lamp of spiritual light is the perfect image of yourself.

Transform your energies into redemptive goodness and understanding towards everyone, spending the oil of your goodwill in selflessness and sacrifice, and your life, in Christ, will really start to shine.

~ 82 ~

The One Who Serves Goes Forward

"For the Son of Man did not come to be served, but to serve." – Jesus. (Mk. 10:45)

All over the world, nature is a divine laboratory that uses the spirit of work as the normal means of evolution.

Conscientious eyes can see cooperation and assistance in the simplest manifestations of the lower kingdoms.

The soil serves the seed. The seed enriches humankind.

The breeze helps the blossoms by carrying their life principles from one to another. Blossoms then produce blessed fruit.

Rivers flow to the sea. The sea produces rain-bearing clouds.

At the present level of evolution, thousands of animals die every hour on earth by giving meat and blood in order to maintain human life.

We may infer from such struggle that work is the price for the redemptive or sanctifying journey.

People that are used to being waited on all the time do not know what to do when alone.

On the other hand, those who serve for the pleasure of being useful are always progressing and they find a thousand resources within themselves for the solution to every problem.

The former are at a standstill.

The latter evolve.

Those who complain excessively about others because they are unaware of the effort needed to meet everyday necessities end up being enslaved to those who serve them, thus their day is ruined if they cannot find someone to set their table. But those who learn to serve know how to minimize problems and find new alternatives.

Followers of the Gospel who do not reap the joy of helping their neighbor are very far from true discipleship because faithful friends of the Good News know that Jesus came to serve, and they dedicate themselves on behalf of everyone until the end of the struggle.

If there is more joy in giving than in receiving, there is more happiness in serving than in being served.

The one who serves goes forward.

83

Let Us Go Further

Therefore, leaving the elementary teachings about Christ behind, let us go on to maturity, not re-laying the foundation of repentance from acts that lead to death... – Paul. (Heb. 6:1)

Accepting the power of Jesus, remaining certain of one's own resurrection after death, and comforting oneself with the benefits of faith, constitute a rudimentary phase in learning about the Gospel.

Practicing the lessons we have learned by associating them with our everyday lives represents the living and sanctifying course.

The student that never goes beyond reciting the alphabet will never penetrate the luminous mental realm of the great masters.

It is not enough to place our soul at the door of the temple and kneel reverently; we have to return to our usual pathways and manifest within ourselves the principles of redemptive faith, thus sublimating our everyday lives.

What would we say about a worker that only went up to the door of his workshop and praised its greatness, without dedicating himself to the work it demands?

What would we say about an admirably equipped ship that remained in port without ever sailing?

There are thousands of believers in the Good News in this lamentable position of stagnation. They are usually persons who are correct regarding all the rudimentary principles of Christ's Doctrine. They believe, they worship, they console themselves faultlessly, but they do not progress in order to become wiser and nobler. From the human point of view, they do not know how to act, to struggle or to suffer when alone.

In order to counteract such problems, Paul states with profound wisdom: "Leaving the elementary teachings about the doctrine of Jesus behind, let us go on to perfection, not repenting over and over again; otherwise we are nothing more than authors of dead works."

Therefore, let us not be like students who study and study … but who never learn how to harmonize themselves with the lesson, and let us also remember that if repentance is useful from time to time, repenting over and over is a sign of stubbornness and weakness.

ns 84 ns

Instruments

How will one know what is being played on the flute or sitar? – Paul. (1 Cor. 14:7)

Christian workers should all consider themselves to be instruments in the hands of the Divine Master, so that the sublime harmony of the Gospel may be irreprehensible for the complete victory of the Good.

However, although the unlimited wisdom of the Heavenly Sender remains sovereign and perfect, earthly receivers show lamentable deficiencies.

One has faith, but cannot tolerate his neighbor's imperfections.

Another endures with Christian charity the weaknesses of her brothers and sisters, but does not have the strength to control her own impulses.

Another is benevolent and trustworthy, but avoids study and meditation in favor of ignorance.

Still another is imaginative and enthusiastic, but subtly avoids actually doing physical work.

This one is an excellent counselor, but does not sanctify her own actions.

That one is an outstanding doctrinal preacher, but is also fond of telling undignified stories, with which he shows irreverence for the Revelation he bears.

There is yet another that observes physical chastity, but cannot control her ambition for easy money.

And lastly, there is one that has managed to detach himself from gold, land, houses and delicacies, but feeds a veritable fire in the flesh.

One cannot argue about our imperfection as followers of the Good News.

That is why we are still learners.

The planet is not a finished paradise, and we are very far from angelhood.

However, obeying, managing, teaching or fighting, it is essential that we tune our instrument of endeavor to the diapason of the Master if we do not wish to impair his works.

Let us avoid the unsure, indistinct or disturbing performance of our tasks, offering him our complete goodwill in whatever we do, and the Divine Kingdom will manifest itself more quickly wherever we may be.

85

Obstacles

Let us throw off every impediment and sin that surrounds us, and let us run with perseverance the race before us. – Paul. (Heb. 12:1)

The great apostle to the Gentiles describes the Christian endeavor as a race of the soul in the grand stadium of life.

Of course, by resorting to this image he had the Greek games of his time in mind, and so, without mentioning the enthusiasm and the healthy emulation that should preside over such an effort, let us recall only the initial act of the competitors.

Each participant would shed his usual outer clothing in order to compete, wearing apparel that was as light as possible.

Thus, in the acquisition of eternal life, it is also crucial for us to rid ourselves of the clothing that suffocates the spirit.

Our hearts must be made light by eliminating every useless burden.

In the light of the Good News, disciples find themselves before the Master, clothed in sanctifying obligations towards all people.

Impediments to a victorious race appear almost every day. We frequently have to face them even in the least significant moments of our lives.

An unexpected obstacle arises every hour.

It may be the cold and intolerant family member.

It may be the dryness of the hearts around us.

It may be the husband that abandoned the family.

It may be the wife who ran off to pursue inferior objectives.

It may be the friend who deluded himself on the islands of rest and relaxation, deciding to put off his journey for a while.

It may be the coworker that was taken away by death.

It may be gratuitous hatred.

It may indifference towards the appeals of the Good.

Pursuit by ill-will.

The torment of strife.

The Good News, however, offers Christians the victory of divine glory.

If we want to reach the finish line, let us put all obstacles aside and persevere in the race of love and light before us.

~ 86 ~

Are You Sick?

And the prayer offered in faith will heal the sick person; the Lord will raise him up.
(James 5: 15)

Everyone gets sick; nevertheless, very few stop to ponder true healing.

If you yourself are sick, do not believe that taking medication orally or through the pores can restore you to full health.

A pill may help, and an injection may make you feel better, but never forget that real sicknesses proceed from the soul.

The mind is a creative source.

Little by little, life molds around you what you desire.

Of what use is external medication if you continue to be unhappy, discouraged or rebellious?

Perhaps you have asked human doctors or spiritual benefactors to help you, but at the very first sign of improvement, you abandoned the medication or wholesome counsel and returned to the very same abuses that caused your infirmity in the first place.

How can you hope to regenerate your health if you spend all your time being angry or discouraged? Occasional indignation, when just and constructive for the general interest, is always a good thing, as long as we use it in the service of spiritual growth. However, daily indignation directed at everyone, everything, and even ourselves, is a pernicious habit that brings unforeseen consequences.

Discouragement is like an anesthetic that benumbs and destroys.

And what about slander or idleness, when you spend your precious time on fruitless conversation, thus draining your energies?

What miraculous genie can give you organic balance if you do not know how to remain silent or forgive, if you do not help others and try to understand them, if you do not humble yourself before the higher designs, or if you do not seek to live in harmony with others?

No matter how quickly help from the earthly or spirit plane may rush to your side, you continue to waste your energies and become a thoughtless victim of indirect suicide.

Therefore, if you are sick, my friend, learning to pray and understand, helping others and preparing your heart for the Great Change is more important than any medication.

Rid yourself of the transitory things that the Divine Power has loaned you in accordance with the Law of Usage, and remember that sooner or later you will return to the Greater Life, where we always face our own conscience.

Avoid being mean.

Enrich your own qualities of personal sympathy by practicing fraternal love.

Seek intimacy with wisdom by means of study and meditation.

Do not stain your pathway.

Serve always.

Work to promote the Good.

Hold loyally to the higher ideal that illumines your heart and remain convinced that if you cultivate the prayer of a living faith at every step, either here or in the beyond, the Lord will raise you up.

~ 87 ~

Did You Receive the Light?

Did you receive the Holy Spirit when you believed? (Acts 19:2)

Catholics receive the sacrament of Baptism along with a personal identification seal that is kept in the records of the church to which they belong.

Protestants undergo the same ceremony and receive a religious registration number in the church they attend.

Spiritists join this or that entity that is dedicated to our Consoling Doctrine and then verbally participate in its renewing endeavor.

All these students of the Christian School rejoice and are comforted.

Some of them share the happiness of the Eucharistic Table, which keeps their hope in heaven alive; others sing together, praising the Divine Goodness, receiving resources of encouragement for the sanctifying journey; still others gather in ardent prayer and receive luminous, revealing messages from heavenly messengers who consolidate their faith in immortality, beyond...

All these approaches have their benefits, advantages and consolation.

However, it is crucial to realize that although the seed is helped by fertilization, water and sun, it must do an inner working in order to be productive.

Therefore, ponder the sublimity of the apostolic question: Did you receive the Holy Spirit when you believed?

Use the revelation with which faith blesses and sanctifies your way, spreading the Good.

Your life may become a fountainhead of blessings for your soul and for others if you truly dedicate yourself to the Master of Love. Remember that it is not you who waits for the Divine Light; rather, it is the Divine Light, the power of heaven at your side, which waits for you.

~ 88 ~

Coming to One's Senses

"When he came to his senses..." – (Lk. 15:17)

This little excerpt from the parable of the prodigal son awakens invaluable considerations about life.

Judas dreamed about the political domination of the Gospel. He was interested in the compulsory transformation of people. Nonetheless, when he finally came to his senses, it was too late, because the Divine Friend had already been delivered into the hands of cruel judges.

Other characters of the Good News came to their senses in time to accomplish soul-saving rectification.

Mary Magdalene had placed her inner life in the hands of wicked spirits, but when she came to her senses, under the influence of Christ, she realized how much time she had wasted, and she attained the loftiest spiritual worthiness through humility and selflessness.

Intimidated by threats of persecution and suffering, Peter denied the Divine Master.

However, when he came to his senses at a compassionate look from Jesus, he wept bitterly and advanced resolutely in the apostolate for his rehabilitation.

Paul gave himself over to insane passion against Christianity, and furiously persecuted any and every manifestation of the nascent Gospel. Nonetheless, as soon as he came to his senses before the sublime call of the Lord, he repented of his wrongs and became one of the most brilliant collaborators of the triumph of Christianity.

There are many, many believers of every kind in the most diverse areas of the faith; nevertheless, trouble and doubt reign amongst them because they live immersed in purely verbal interpretations of the heavenly revelation, in superficial delights, in the illusion of the flesh, or imprudently attached to the materialistic life. For them, joy means immediate satisfaction of a want, and peace is the temporary sensation of the body's physical well-being, without any pain, in order to be able to eat and drink without any hindrances.

Therefore, come to your senses under the blessing of Jesus, and then, leaving inactivity behind and embracing the incessant endeavor of your redemption, you will be surprised at how different life has become.

~ 89 ~

On Our Journey

Jesus asked him, "What would you like me to do for you?" – (Mk. 10:51)

Each student has a lesson to learn.

Each worker has been entrusted with a task.

Each vase has its usefulness.

Each struggler has an ordeal to endure.

Thus, each of us has our own individual testimony on the road of life.

We often fail at our commitments and thus greatly increase our debts. Yet, in our redemptive endeavor, we beg the Lord for his mercy, compassion and help.

The question the Master asks of the blind man from Jericho is highly meaningful, however.

"What would you like me to do for you?"

This question shows us that the beggar's delicate position was in line with the imperatives of the Law.

Nothing happens *in absentia* of the Divine Principles.

Blind Bartimaeus knew how to respond and asked to be able to see. Nevertheless, how many people pray for access to the Savior's presence, but when asked by him, they answer it their own detriment?

Let us remember that sometimes we may have to lose our earthly home in order to learn the way to our heavenly home. On many occasions, we are abandoned by those we love the most so that we may return to the divine bonds. And then there are the times when the wounds of the body are called on to heal those of the spirit, and there are situations in which paralysis teaches us how precious being able to move is.

It is natural for us to ask for the Master's help in our afflictions and difficulties; meanwhile, let us not forget to work for the Good on the most painful passages of rectification and ascension, convinced that we invariably find ourselves in the most just, beneficial and deserved opportunity of work, and that maybe, for the time being, we do not know how to choose anything better.

~ 90 ~

Courageously

Be on your guard; stand firm in the faith; act courageously; be strong. – Paul (1 Cor. 16:13)

Be on your guard in the daily struggle.
Stand firm in the faith when faced with the storm.
Act courageously in every difficult situation.
Be strong in suffering in order to receive its lesson of light.

Still today, Paul's advice to the Corinthians is clothed in surprising appropriateness.

In order for us to receive the substantial qualities of redemption, we must have the courage of those who trust in the Lord and in themselves.

A flood of unreasonable tears is worthless before a wrong that has been committed.

It is our duty to repent of any evil we may have done, but to continuously feel sorry about it is wasting our time in redeeming it. Of course, deliberate evil is a crime; however, a thoughtless wrong is a valuable lesson as long as we incline ourselves to the Lord's designs.

Without moral resistance in the storm of purifying conflicts, even the noblest heart falls apart.

Therefore, we cannot rest in our endeavor of spiritual growth.

Of course, we will stumble many times.

Of course, we will get scratched by thorns along the way.

Our situation will be regrettable, however, whenever we demand a soft bandage of undue consolations, thus halting our journey to the Almighty.

Christians are not students that allow themselves undeserved rest. Disciples of a Master who served whoever needed him until his final testimony on the cross, they must toil at sowing and harvesting the Infinite Good, being on their guard, helping and acting courageously.

~ 91 ~

Matters of the Heart

...that your love may grow more and more in full knowledge and in all discernment.
– Paul (Phil. 1:9)

Love is the divine power of the universe.

However, we must be on our guard not to wander from the correct use of it.

When people devote themselves wholeheartedly to their perishable coffers, this energy in their heart is called "greed"; when they constantly worry about defending their possessions, believing them to be the center of their life wherever they are, this same energy becomes "selfishness"; when they only see reasons to praise what they themselves represent, do, and feel, with obvious disregard for other peoples' values, the sentiment that predominates is called "envy."

Paul, writing to the loving Philippian community, formulates a far-reaching suggestion. His wish is that "love may grow more and more in knowledge and discernment so that the disciple may be able to tell what is best."

Therefore, let us learn in order to know.

Let us teach ourselves to discern.

Intellectual learning and moral growth are imperatives for life, enabling us to show love in the realm of sublimation that brings us closer to God.

Let us heed the apostolic advice and grow in spiritual qualities for everlasting life, because many times our love simply means wanting, and wanting, by itself, can thoughtlessly destroy life's most beautiful situations.

92

Signs from Heaven

So they asked him, "What sign will you give that we may see it and believe in you?" (Jn. 6:30)

In every era, when someone on the earth refers to the things of heaven, a veritable multitude of inquirers rushes to ask for objective signs for the truth that is being proclaimed.

Consequently, modern mediums are constantly assailed by the demands of those in search of the spiritual life.

This one is a clairvoyant and should give proof of what he sees.

That one writes under uncommon conditions and is constrained to furnish proof regarding the sources of her inspiration.

Another materializes discarnates and is challenged to do so in public.

However, many people forget that all the Lord's creatures externalize their own particular signs.

The mineral is recognized by its usefulness.

The tree is named by its fruit.

The sky spreads messages of light.

The water gives notice of its incessant work.

The air, without using words, tells of its ability to maintain life.

And the same imperatives apply as far as men and women are concerned.

Each brother or sister in the struggle is examined according to his or her characteristics.

Fools are known by their puerilities.

Wise people manifest prudence.

Those who are the best at what they do demonstrate the virtues that are peculiar to them.

Thus, when asking for revelations from heaven regarding their earthly pilgrimage, learners of the Gospel should not neglect the necessity to demonstrate they are firmly disposed to progressing to heaven.

There was a day when a crowd asked the Savior, who had already done great things for them: "What sign will you give that we may see it and believe in you?"

So, just think that if such a question was asked of the Lord of Life, what sort of question will the Most High ask us every time we pray for signs from heaven in order for us to fulfill our simple task?

93

The Inner Altar

We have an altar ... – Paul. (Heb. 13:10)

To this day, we have built altars far and wide in praise of the Master and Lord.

Made of gold, marble, wood or clay, adorned with perfumes, treasures and flowers, we have raised sanctuaries and have called on the help of art in adding artificial illumination and external beauty.

As soon as the monument to faith is finished, we get down on our knees in prayer and search for divine inspiration.

And in fact, every such activity is praiseworthy, even when we make the common mistake of forgetting those starving out on the street and focus on the pomp of worship, because love and gratitude to the Power of Heaven, even when wrongly expressed, deserves veneration.

However, it is indispensable to grow into the Greater Life.

The Master himself used the Samaritan woman to warn us that the time would come when the Father would be worshiped in spirit and in truth.

Paul adds that we have an altar.

The ultimate purpose of temples of stone is to awaken our awareness.

Awakened Christians, however, act as self-priests, glorifying love when faced with hatred, peace when faced with strife, peace-of-mind when faced with trouble, good when faced with evil...

Therefore, let us remember our inner altar, which we should consecrate to the Divine Power and to Heavenly Goodness.

Coming to stone altars with a soul shut to the light and to the inspiration of the Master is the same as setting an impenetrable coffer of darkness out in the full light of the sun. The light waves continue to be light waves, but the darkness is not affected.

Hence, let us present our oblations and sacrifices to the Lord by means of blessed gifts of love for our neighbor, thus worshipping the Lord on the altar of our heart; and let us proceed with the work we are called to do.

94

The Helmet of Hope

Having the hope of salvation as a helmet. –
Paul (1 Thess. 5:8)

The helmet is protection for the head, in which life has placed the seat of the manifestation of thought, and Paul could not have used a more suitable symbol for the Christian mind than the helmet as the hope of salvation.

If the sentiments are often subject to attacks of violent rage, the reason often experiences the assault of discouragement when faced with the struggle for the victory of the Good. This must never happen.

Forces that oppose the Gospel of salvation shoot rays of anesthetizing negativity at the enthusiasm of learners.

The demands of everybody and the indifference of many may try to crystalize the disciple's energy, dispersing his or her noble impulses or neutralizing his or her ideals of renewal.

However, it is crucial to always expect the development of latent principles of the Good, even as evil – which is temporary – sends its roots in all directions.

It is crucial to anticipate the strengthening of the weak, just as a farmer cannot lose faith in the tender shoots, and to wait for joy and courage from the downcast with the same expectation of a floriculturist who relies on the manifestation of aroma and beauty in his or her garden full of leafless stems.

But it is also crucial to realize that Christian serenity does not mean failing to act in order to continuously improve people, things and situations in every aspect of the way.

That is perhaps why the apostle does not use the symbol of a protective hat.

A hat almost always implies going for a stroll, enjoying leisure and rest, when it is not a part of the overall outfit, according to the fashion of the time.

A helmet, however, is a defensive piece of equipment used for battle.

And Jesus' disciples are effective combatants against evil. They do not have much time to think about themselves or to demand a lot of time off, because they know that the Master himself is still hard at work.

Therefore, let us keep our minds on the helmet of faith-filled hope and press on to the supreme victory of the Good.

95

See and Go Forward

"One thing I do know: I was blind but now I see!"
(Jn. 9:25)

Despite the renewing work of the Gospel in the areas of consolation and preaching, which is unfolding before the masses, sowing miracles of comfort in people's souls, the subtle and nearly unknown endeavor of making use of the Good News is always individual and non-transferable.

As they go about their daily lives on their journey of spiritual learning, if Christians do not enjoy noticeable advantages according to human, immediate standards – advantages such as consolation, encouragement or material prosperity – so as to apply the living teachings of Jesus in their own lives, they are seen as peculiar, often times by their own fellow workers in ministry.

Having reached such a position, and if they can take advantage of the sublime opportunity by means of submission and diligence, they experience a complete change of behavior.

They change the table of values that surrounds them.

They know where the eternal fundamentals are hidden.

New areas of struggle open up to them through an inner vision that others cannot understand.

They discover different motives for spiritual growth through personal sacrifice, and they recognize loftier sources of incentive for their endeavor.

Consequently they frequently provoke heated discussions concerning their attitude towards Jesus.

As they grasp the Master's teachings more clearly, they are seen as fanatic, backward, stupid or crazy.

However, if you really are seeking redemption with the Lord, then go forward with self-confidence. Regard without affliction or discouragement the attacks by incomprehensible and stagnated hearts brought on by your genuine, Jesus-focused activity. Repeat the words of the blind man who received his sight, and go forward.

ns 96 ns

Go beyond what Others Do

"Do not tax collectors do the same?" –
Jesus. (Mt. 5:46)

To work diligently every day; to mind one's duties in the home; to do what one is required by law to do; and to act rightly by doing our utmost to fulfill our immediate responsibilities: these are things that pertain to both believers and unbelievers in everyday life.

Jesus, however, expects more from his disciples.

Are you in tune with the imperatives of your daily work, spreading courage, joy and interest all around you?

Do you know how to sew the Good where others have proven to be fruitless?

Do you know how to successfully use materials that others have already deemed useless?

Do you wait patiently where others have given up in despair?

As a believer, do you continue your spirit of service where unbelievers have stopped theirs?

Do you share your friends' joy without envy or jealously, and do you share in the suffering of your adversaries without a false feeling of superiority or pride?

What can you give of yourself to the ministry of charity?

To ensure the continuity of the species, to be useful to all, and to adapt to the activities of life are things that even the animals do.

For many millennia, ordinary people have been eating, drinking, sleeping and acting without making fundamental changes in society. However, a blessed light has shone on the earth for the last twenty centuries, spreading Christ's teachings and inviting us to ascend to the peaks of higher spirituality. But not everyone realizes this, although it does involve everyone. Even so, for those who delight in its extraordinary blessings, the Master's challenge issues forth, asking us what we are doing that is out of the ordinary.

97

The Message of the Cross

For the message of the cross is foolishness to those who are perishing, but to us who are saved it is the power of God. – Paul (1 Cor. 1:18)

The message of the cross has always been dolorous.

A voice that was at first disagreeable and incomprehensible descended from Calvary to the world.

The Master's martyrdom held all the arguments for a superficially complete denial of it.

Complete abandonment by the ones he loved the most.

Dreadful thirst.

Irreversible surrender.

Spontaneous forgiveness that expressed total humiliation.

Sarcasm and ridicule between two thieves.

Defeat with having put up a fight.

An infamous death.

However, Christ uses this apparent failure to teach the way of Eternal Resurrection, showing that the "self" can never approach God without moral growth and purification.

Even today, the message of the cross is foolishness to those who remain forever in the circles of reincarnations of low-level spiritually. Such persons intend to do nothing but conspire with death, exterminating the loveliest blossoms of the sentiments. They control many, but are incapable of self-control. They accumulate the wealth that foolishness has thrown away, and they weave dark threads of stubborn passions, into which they fall without realizing it, just like a spider caught in its own web.

If we repeat the message of the cross to our brothers and sisters who are drowning in the flesh, they will call us insane. But all of us, who, due to the warnings of a renewing faith, have been saved from worse falls, are told that, during the bitterest trials, the disciple goes to the Master, just as the Master went to the Father in the hidden glory of the crucifixion.

~ 98 ~

The Breastplate of Charity

Let us be temperate, putting on the breastplate of faith and charity. – Paul. (1 Thes. 5:8)

Paul was infinitely wise when he advised workers of the light to put on the breastplate of charity.

For the success desired in our mission of love in the company of Christ, the most important thing is to protect one's heart.

If we do not cloak the source of our sentiments with vibrations of ardent love, utilizing a high level of comprehension in the areas of the sanctifying experience in which we struggle in the earthly arena, it will be very difficult to accomplish the task that the Lord has entrusted to us.

Frequent irritation when faced with ignorance only postpones the advantages of our beneficent teaching.

Excessive indignation when faced with weakness only destroys the fragile seeds of virtue.

Frequent anger in the daily struggle may increase the number of our enemies without any benefit to the work to which we have devoted ourselves.

Excessive strictness when faced with persons who do not know the benefits of discipline may produce counterproductive effects due to a lack of education in that particular environment.

Thus, understanding that Christians are in a veritable state of struggle, and that at times we are challenged by suggestions of intemperate irritation, inappropriate indignation, unjustifiable anger, or destructive strictness, the Apostle to the Gentiles prescribes the breastplate of charity as a protective sentinel for the central organs of the expression of life.

It is crucial to arm the heart with infinite fraternal understanding in order to focus on our ministry.

Conviction and the enthusiasm of faith are enough for a good start, but in order to continue our ministry and finish it successfully, we cannot do without patient, kindly and invincible charity.

~ 99 ~

Persevere and Press On

Therefore, lift up your weary arms and weak knees. – Paul. (Heb. 12:12)

Negligent farmers often heed the suggestions of weariness. They may stop working because a storm and flood ruins their crop and robs them of their insipient will to go on. They rest because of the calluses that the hoe has given them, and so worms wind up destroying their crop.

At first they work hard but they cannot "lift up their arms" to persevere with their work; consequently, they lose the harvest.

Travelers, in their turn, may not reach the end of their journey on time if they are not careful. They complain about the heat and rest in the shade of illusory shelters, where unexpected perils may strike them. At other times, they point to their bloody feet and lie down on the side of the road and become a common beggar.

They have healthy knees, but they are not willing to use them because they are tired and hurt, so they miss out on the joy of reaching their destination.

So it is with our spiritual journey.
Struggle is the means.
Spiritual growth is the end.
Disillusionment causes bitterness.
Difficulty complicates things.
Ingratitude hurts.
Malice wounds.

However, if we abandon the field of the heart because we cannot lift up our hands again in persevering effort, the worms of discouragement will soon thrive in the midst of our dearest hopes; and if we do not want to press on because our knees are tired, we might be waylaid by the shade of false shelters for centuries.

~ 100 ~

Absentees

Now Thomas, one of the Twelve, was not with them when Jesus appeared. – (Jn. 20:24)

Thomas was dissatisfied and demanded proof because he had not witnessed Jesus' first visit after his death; thus, he became a symbol for all learners who are unconcerned about their obligations.

What happened to the absent disciple happens to all workers who ignore their duties.

Spiritual growth, with its blessings of light, is also an instructional course.

Students who enroll in school but then constantly skip classes only abuse the institution, because merely enrolling does not mean they are taking advantage of their classes. Unless they learn the alphabet, students will never be able to put words together, and without words, they will never be able to put a sentence together.

An identical process applies to the evolution of the spirit.

How can believers receive divine grace if they ignore their duties towards their closest neighbors? If they avoid contact with the humble obligations of each day, how can they enlarge their sentiments in order to adapt to the eternal glories?

Thomas was not with his friends when the Master appeared. Consequently, he complained, creating the model for the doubtful, demanding disciple.

In endeavors of spiritual growth, the matter is analogous.

Individuals enroll in the school of the superior life, but instead of dedicating themselves to their daily lessons, they prove to be mere applicants for immediate advantages.

They are usually not with other workers when Jesus comes, so they immediately complain and despair.

Logic, however, never abandons the straight pathway.

Whoever wants the divine blessing must work in order to deserve it.

Learners who skip class cannot expect to benefit from the lesson.

~ 101 ~

The Veil of "Self"

For everyone searches for what is his own and not for what is Jesus Christ's. – Paul. (Phil. 2:21)

We do, in fact, study with Christ the divine science of connecting ourselves with the Father, but we are still a long ways from a genuine communion with the divine interests.

From behind of the veil of "self," we hold on to a regretful blindness in the presence of life.

Let us impartially examine our characteristic attitudes as we serve the Good – of which we are beginning coworkers – and we will see that even there, in virtue-related issues, our amount of individual caprice is invariably enormous.

The ancient legend of Narcissus is very much alive to some degree in our smallest gestures.

In everything and everywhere, we are in love with our own image.

We usually love ourselves in our dearest loved ones because, if they express points of view that are different than ours, even if they are superior, we instinctively feel less affection towards them.

Regarding our endeavors for the Good, we especially love the methods and procedures that derive from our own way of being and thinking, because, if the work evolves and improves, reflecting the thoughts of other people instead of our own, then almost imperceptibly we lose interest in it.

We accept collaboration from others, but we find it difficult to offer our own.

If we are in a superior position, we happily donate a fortune to the needy brother or sister who is beneath us so that we may lustily relish our fine, upstanding qualities in the acknowledgement he or she will be constrained to offer us for a long time, but we rarely give a smile of goodwill to someone who is richer or stronger and who has been put right in front of us by the Divine Designs.

At every step of the human struggle, we find virtue surrounded by vice, and that worthwhile knowledge is almost always suffocated by the thorns of ignorance because unfortunately, each one of us usually seeks his or her own 'self.'

Nevertheless, thanks to God's goodness, suffering and death overtake us in the experience of the body and beyond it, snatching us away to vast lands of meditation and humility, where, for our true happiness within the glory of living, we gradually learn to search for what belongs to Jesus Christ.

// 102

Let Us Be Joyful Always

Be joyful always. – Paul. (1 Thess. 5:16)

This New Testament text does not exhort us to rejoice only on days when we feel personally happy.

It simply says, "Be joyful always."

There is nothing in the world that cannot be seen as a respectable reason for work, joy and satisfaction.

Even nature itself exhibits obvious teachings in this respect every day.

For instance, after the gale that uproots and mutilates trees, destroys nests and covers roads with mud, a new sowing appears, the tree trunk produces new branches, birds rebuild their homes and the road is crowned with sunlight.

Only human beings, those heroes of intelligence, hold on to the grimace of pessimism for an undetermined time, as if they were angry and disillusioned geniuses bent on destroying what does not belong to them.

A continued lack of hope and joy in the soul points to deficient evolution.

There are invitations to spiritual growth and improvement everywhere, challenging us to act for the common good.

Nobody is so unhappy that he or she cannot produce a few thoughts of goodness, nor so poor that he or she cannot distribute a few smiles and kind words with his or her companions in the daily struggle.

Being downhearted all the time is like rust in the gears of the soul. Endless complaining is laziness or destructive resistance.

It is necessary to awaken our heart and worthily attend to what we are responsible for in the evolutionary drama of life, without hatred, without complaint, without discouragement.

Life is what it is.

Our companions in it are what they are.

Each one of us receives the portion of struggle necessary for our learning experience. No one is bereft of opportunities to grow.

The main issue is to obey God, loving him and willingly serving one's neighbor. Those who have solved such a problem within themselves know that all people and all situations on life's pathway are living messages by which we may reap blessings of love and wisdom if we accept the lesson the Lord is offering us.

Therefore, let us not forget that Paul, the intrepid warrior of the Gospel, enduring the torment of preoccupations, found the means within himself to tell his brothers and sisters of the struggle: "Be joyful always."

103

Waiting and Receiving

And so after waiting patiently, he received what was promised. – Paul. (Heb. 6:15)

The hope of attaining divine peace involving unchangeable happiness vibrates in all individuals.

The desire of the patriarchs of old is similar to that of modern men and women.

A home crowned with blessings.

A job well-done.

An uplifted conscience.

A higher ideal properly realized.

A triumphant endeavor.

A plentiful harvest.

The soul's aspirations are always the same everywhere.

However, waiting means persisting tirelessly, and receiving means triumphing decidedly.

Between the objective and the goal, it is imperative to start making a continuous and sustained effort right now.

Hope does not mean not doing anything.

And patience means peaceable tenacity in doing the work we propose to do.

If you intend to materialize your purposes with Christ, then keep the formula of patience as the sole open door to victory.

Is there suffering in your tortured dreams? Are your wishes misunderstood by many? Have ingratitude and pain visited your spirit?

Do not waste time weeping, nor curse your problems.

Wait for the surprises of time, acting without hurry.

If each night is new darkness, each day is new light.

Remember that not all waters are the same depth, nor are all trees the same height, girth or species.

Recall the words of the Apostle to the Gentiles.

Waiting patiently, we will receive what was promised.

Do not forget that a sure success does not belong to the one who attacks it, but to the one who knows how to act, persevere and wait for it.

~ 104 ~

In the Presence of the Crowd

Now Jesus, seeing the crowd, went up on a mountain. – (Mt. 5:1)

Cultured people's attitudes towards others will improve as the Gospel enters their hearts.

Unfortunately, so far, very rarely has the crowd received fair treatment by great human personalities.

Many ascend the mountain of authority, fortune, intelligence and power merely to humiliate or forget the crowd afterwards.

Countless priests enrich themselves with learning in order to subject the crowd to their wishes.

Cunning politicians exploit the crowd's passions to their own advantage.

Tyrants disguised as leaders poison the crowd's souls and lead it to the brink of destruction, like shepherds who divide their flock for slaughter.

Judges who are ill-prepared for their dignifying duties confuse the crowd's reasoning.

Unscrupulous administrators use the crowd's numerical advantages to create effects that are contrary to progress.

Down through time, we have seen the work of genuine missionaries of the Good being harmed by ignorance, which causes troubles and fears amidst the crowd.

However, for the community of learners of the Gospel, the standard of Jesus shines sovereignly in every environment of faith.

Seeing the crowd, the Master goes up on a mountain and begins to teach.

It is indispensable to employ our energies in the service of education.

Let us help people to think, grow and become better persons.

Helping everyone so that they may be benefitted and uplifted to the same degree as we want improvement and prosperity for ourselves constitutes real and essential happiness for us.

To the east, west, north and south of our individuality, there are thousands of people in worse conditions than ours.

Let us stretch out our arms, expand our hearts and send emanations of understanding, fraternity and kindness, helping them unconditionally.

When Christians pronounce the sacred words, "Our Father," they are not only acknowledging the Fatherhood of God, but accepting all humankind as their family.

~ 105 ~

You Are the Light

"You are the light of the world." –
Jesus. (Mt. 5:14)

When Christ told his disciples that they were the light of the world, he conferred a tremendous responsibility on them.

The mission of light is to illuminate roads, scatter darkness and save lives, a mission that is invariably carried out at the cost of the fuel that feeds it.

The candle flame burns the liquefied wax of the wick.

The electric light consumes power from the substation.

And light, whether from the sun or from the candelabra, is always a message of security, discernment, comfort and joy for those upon whom they shine.

Therefore, if we are to grasp Christ's lesson and are interested in following him, then we must be willing to donate our energies to the ongoing activity of the Good so that the Good News may shine on the pathway of redemption for all.

Christians that do not have a spirit of selflessness are like a dead torch in the sanctuary of the Gospel.

Let us seek the Lord, offering the best of ourselves to others.

Let us follow him, helping others indiscriminately.

Let us not get entangled in conflicts or pointless inquiries.

"You are the light of the world," our Master has exhorted us; and the light does not argue but clarifies, aids, helps and illuminates.

~ 106 ~

Let Us Serve the Good

The light shines in the darkness... – (Jn. 1:5)

Do not feel afflicted because you seem to be alone as you serve the Good.

Jesus, too, was alone before bringing his companions together for the apostolic endeavor. He was alone, facing a vast world, like a farmer who has no tools with which to work to clear an immense forest...

Nevertheless, Christianity emerged as a living temple of love, and it is still under construction for human happiness.

Jesus, however, despite knowing the power of the truth that he brought with him, did not use his superiority to humiliate or hurt anyone.

Above all his other concerns, he invariably sought the Good in every situation and in everyone.

He did not waste time on inappropriate criticisms.

He did not engage in pointless arguments.

He established the redemptive kingdom of which he was the messenger, serving and loving, always helping and supporting each lesson with his own exemplification.

Therefore, let us continue on our redemptive march ahead, even when we feel alone.

Above all, let us serve the Good, but avoid arguments and bad situations where evil can expand itself.

Flee the darkness for the radiance of the light.

Let us remember that, even though thousands of miles of darkness in the middle of the night cannot quench even a half inch of the shining flame of a candle, all it takes is a puff of wind to extinguish it.

~ 107 ~

Let Us Renew Ourselves Each Day

Be transformed by the renewing of your mind so that you can prove what is the good, pleasing and perfect will of God. – Paul. (Rom. 12.2)

The apparent transformation of our personality on the outside does no good.

More titles, more financial resources, more potential for comfort, and better social possibilities can merely increase our responsibilities.

Let us renew ourselves on the inside.

We must advance in superior knowledge even if it costs us sweat and tears.

Accepting the problems of the world and overcoming them by means of the power of our labor and serenity is the best formula for acquiring discernment.

Pain, sacrifice, affliction and suffering are processes of sublimation that the Greater World offers us so that our spiritual vision may increase.

Material comforts often stagnate our minds if we cannot overcome the fascinating perils of worldly advantages.

Let us renew ourselves each day by studying the lessons of the pioneers of progress and by living under the inspiration of incessant service.

Let us apply ourselves to building a balanced life wherever we may be, but let us not forget that it is only by fulfilling our duties in the concretization of the Good that we can grasp what life is, and with it, the understanding of what God's perfect will for us is.

~ 108 ~

A Little Yeast

Don't you know that a little yeast causes the whole batch of dough to rise? – Paul. (1 Cor. 5:6)

Nobody lives alone.

Our soul is always a center of influence for others.

Our deeds possess a language all their own.

Our words act at a distance.

We find ourselves magnetically associated with one another.

Actions and reactions characterize our progress.

Therefore, we need to know what kind of forces we are projecting on those around us.

Our conduct is an open book.

How many of our insignificant gestures impact our neighbor, causing unexpected resolutions!

How many of our apparently meaningless utterances cause great events to happen!

Each day we emit suggestions for either good or ill…

Leaders lead followers.

Servers inspire administrators.

What is the pathway our attitude is pointing out?

A little yeast causes the whole lump of dough to rise.

We do not have the means to analyze the extent of our influence, but we can examine its essential quality.

Thus, be careful about the invisible nourishment that you are feeding the lives around you.

Destiny discloses itself to us in currents of inflow and outflow. The forces that are exteriorized by our activities today will return to the center of our activities tomorrow.

~ 109 ~

Christ's Example

...for he knew what was in a man. (Jn. 2:25)

Yes, Jesus knew what was in men and women, but he never let himself be influenced negatively.

He knew that usury lived with Zacchaeus, but he led him from miserliness to generosity.

He knew that Mary Magdalene was possessed by evil spirits, but he renewed her for pure love.

He recognized the intellectual vanity of Nicodemus, but he gave him new concepts about the grandeur and magnificence of life.

He identified the weakness of Simon Peter, but little by little he installed in the disciple's heart a spiritual strength that would make him the pillar of newly-born Christianity.

He saw the doubts of Thomas, but never forsook him.

He knew the darkness that dwelled in Judas, but he did not deny him his affection.

Above all, Jesus was concerned with providing each soul a broader vision of life, and in allotting to each spirit effective resources for renewal for the Good.

Therefore, do not condemn your neighbor because you can see his or her imperfections.

Following Christ's example, help as many people as you can.

The Divine Friend knows what is in us ... He knows the dark and heavy burden of our past, the difficulties of our present, full of hesitations and wrongs; nevertheless, he lovingly holds out his hands to us.

~ 110 ~

Let Us Watch and Pray

"Watch and pray so that you do not fall into temptation." – Jesus. (Mt. 26:41)

The most terrible temptations come from the profound darkness of our individuality, just as the darkest muck, capable of darkening a lake, comes from its own bottom.

For the tasks of readjustment, we are reborn on the earth with imbalances from our past.

Within the roots of our own tendencies, we find the liveliest suggestions of an inferior quality. In our relationship with our family members, we are faced with the strongest causes of discord and struggle.

Within our very selves, we may exercise good cheer and patience, faith and humility. In contact with our best friends, we have plenty of learning material to incorporate into our lives the qualities of good-will, forgiveness, pure fraternity and an incessant goodness.

Therefore, do not think you can go through life and not face temptations. They are born with you; they are associated with you, and they are fed by you if you do not combat them decisively, like a farmer who is always willing to co-operate with the land from which he needs to take good seeds.

Going from cradle to grave under the hammers of temptation is completely natural. Facing obstacles, enduring trials, tolerating gratuitous enmities, and passing through floods of tears are logical vicissitudes of the human experience.

Nevertheless, let us remember the Master's teaching, watching and praying so that we may not succumb to temptations, since it is better to weep under the pinpricks of resistance than to smile under the sedatives of the fall.

~ 111 ~

Let Us Strengthen Ourselves

Be strong in the Lord. – Paul. (Eph. 6:10)

There are many people who think they are strong because they:

Have financial resources, which come and go;

Possess lands, which may be transferred from owner to owner;

Possess physical beauty, which glows then passes;

Have important relatives, who may change;

Have an educated mind, which is often deceived, nonetheless;

Are popular, which leads to disillusionment;

Have political power, which time undoes;

Live in an oasis of exclusivist happiness, which the storm destroys.

Yes, there are many people who think they are winning today, but who end up being defeated tomorrow.

However, only the conscience built up in faith by means of duties well-fulfilled in light of the Eternal Laws can remain invulnerable under self-control.

Only those who sacrifice themselves for love find incorruptible security.

Therefore, let us strengthen ourselves in the Lord, and with an upright soul, let us forge ahead in the fulfillment of the endeavor that the Divine Master has entrusted to us.

~ 112 ~

What Am I To Do?

"What am I to do?" – Paul. (Acts 22:10)

Thousands of people approach the Gospel for the inveterate worship of self-indulgence.

How can I stay in control? some ask.

"How can I relax? enquire others.

And the questions keep multiplying, strange, reproachful, incomprehensible...

There are those who ask for cheap comfort while in the flesh; those who demand undue affections; those who long for unconfessable businesses; those who demand resources to make serving peace and the Good more difficult.

The question of the apostle Paul at the moment he is blessed by the Divine Presence is the standard for all learners and followers of the Good News.

The great laborer for the Revelation does not ask to be transferred from earth to heaven, nor does he degenerate into suggestions of favoritism for his personal circle. He does not ask to be exempt from responsibility, nor does he flee the duties of the struggle.

"What am I to do?" he asked Jesus, grasping the importance of the effort for which he would be responsible.

And the Master tells him to get up and sow light and love through selflessness.

If you have been called to the faith, do not ask the Divine Guide for privileges and benefits that may justify your remaining in spiritual stagnation.

With the Lord, let us seek the endeavor that his Infinite Goodness has reserved for us, and let us proceed triumphantly towards our sublime renewal.

~ 113 ~

Let Us Seek the Best

"Why do you look at the speck in your brother's eye?"
– Jesus. (Mt. 7:3)

Even today, the Master's question is clear and opportune.

Very often, those who have a speck in one of their eyes also have bloody feet. After a laborious journey in virtue, they show that their hands have become calloused from the work, and that their heart has been wounded by a thousand blows of ignorance and inexperience.

We absolutely have to get used to looking for the best so that we do not become hoodwinked by our own malice.

Very often, due to our habit of searching for bagatelles, we miss opportunities for great achievements.

Valuable and respectable coworkers are relegated to the wayside by our thoughtlessness in many circumstances simply because they have minor defects or insignificant shadows from the past, which service on behalf of others could cleanse or dissipate.

Knots in the wood do not obstruct the work of the artisan, and stony parts of a field do not keep the farmer from sowing it.

Let us employ the willing brother or sister in the sowing of the Good, and forget about the trifles in his or her life.

What would become of us if Jesus did not forgive our daily wrongs and defections?

And if we hope to evolve, counting on the Lord's benevolence, why should we deny our neighbor his or her trust in the future?

Let us dedicate ourselves to the task the Lord has reserved for us in the spreading of the light and the Good, and let us be convinced that by doing so, the speck that troubles our neighbor's eye, just like the log that obscures ours, will spontaneously dissolve, restoring our happiness and balance by means of continuous renewal.

~ 114 ~

Put Away Your Sword

"Put away your sword ..." –
Jesus. (Jn. 18:11)

War has always been the terror of nations.

A hurricane of unconsciousness, it opens the door to all the monsters of iniquity wherever it appears. What took a civilization laborious centuries of sweat to build only takes war a few furious days to destroy.

During war, carnage and devastation result, compelling people to cruelty and barbarity, by which bitter days of suffering and regeneration appear for the countries that have accepted its madness.

The very same thing happens within ourselves when we declare war against our fellow beings…

By carrying on a dispute against our neighbor, a destroying torrent of sentiments disturbs our heart. Lofty ideals and sublime aspirations that have been nurtured by our spirit for so long, as well as constructions in the present with the future in mind, and plantings of light and love in the soil of our souls, all collapse and disintegrate because imbalance and violence make us tremble and fall in the vibrations of complete selfishness, which we have relegated to the rearguard of our evolution.

Thereafter, we often have to go through many afflictive lifetimes of expiation in order to correct the breaches that have waylaid the ship of our destiny in brief moments of madness.

In our Christian learning experience, let us remember the Lord's word:

"Put away your sword..."

By feeding the war against others, we lose ourselves in outer darkness, forgetting the good fight that we should pursue within ourselves.

Let us make peace with those around us, struggling against the darkness that still disturbs our lives, so that the kingdom of light may dwell in us.

With our lance at the ready, we will never achieve the good we desire.

The Master's cross was shaped like a sword with the blade pointed downwards.

Thus, let us remember that, in sacrificing himself on a symbolic sword that has been rightfully stuck in the ground, Jesus conferred on humankind the blessing of peace, with happiness and renewal.

~ 115 ~

Let Us Remain Loyal

Moreover, those who have been given a trust must prove trustworthy. – Paul. (1 Cor. 4:2)

Let us live each day doing the best we can do.

If you administer, be fair in the distribution of work.

If you legislate, be loyal to the good of all.

If you spread the gifts of faith, do not neglect the souls around you.

If you teach, be clear in what you teach.

If you devote yourself to art, do not distort divine inspiration.

If you heal, do not despise the patient.

If you build, be safe about it.

If you plough the soil, do it joyfully.

If you work in public sanitation, embrace hygiene as your priesthood.

If you have built a family, sublimate it for the blessings of love and light, even if it costs you affliction and sacrifice.

Do not be troubled by unexpected changes, nor be impressed by the apparent victory of those that devote themselves to all sorts of interests except yours.

Remember the Watchful Eye of Divine Providence, which observes every step we take.

Remember that, wherever you are, you live due to the initiative of the Greater Power that oversees our destinies. Let us remain loyal to our obligations. And, working constantly to spread the Good in the area of struggle that life has entrusted to us, let us wait for the Law's new decisions about us, because the Law will lift us up to a higher plane and will sublimate our activities at the best time.

~ 116 ~

Go and Teach

"Therefore, go and teach..." –
Jesus. (Mt. 28:19)

As we ponder the Lord's commandment to his disciples – go and teach – we need to remember that Jesus himself came and taught.

He came from the Heavenly Heights and taught the way of spiritual elevation to those who were stuck in earthly darkness.

Christ could have given this lesson through faithful emissaries ... Or he could have spoken brilliantly, explaining how to do it...

However, in order to teach surely and fruitfully, he preferred to come to the world of human beings and dwell with them in order to show them how to live on the pathway to perfection.

Thus, rather than some other way, he humbled himself and was born in the Manger; he honored work and study in the home, and in public he was the providential brother of all, helping each one according to his or her needs.

It is inarguably correct that Jesus is called the Divine Master.

Not because he had a throne of gold...

Not because he was the owner of the best library in the world...

Not because he merely exalted the correct and irreproachable word...

Not because he ascended the throne of cultural superiority, dictating obligations to his listeners...

But because he lifted up his own heart in fraternal love, and teaching, made himself a benefactor to all those who received his sublime lessons.

He spoke to us about the Eternal Father, and through his selflessness, he showed us the best way to search for him.

So, if you propose to work for the Gospel, remember that speaking, advising and informing are not enough.

"Go and teach," in the words of Christ, means "go and set an example so that others may learn how it should be done."

~ 117 ~

We Have what We Give

"It is more blessed to give than to receive." –
Paul. (Acts 20:35)

When someone refers to the New Testament passage that says that the act of giving is a greater blessing than that of receiving, almost all students of the Good News think of the word "money."

Of course, when we think about material things, there is always more joy in helping than in being helped; nevertheless, we must not forget spiritual gifts, which, emanating from within us, increase the level and intensity of the joy around us.

Those who give reap the happiness of seeing the multiplication of what they have given.

Offer kindness and you will encourage the sowing of fraternity.

Spread the blessing of forgiveness and you will strengthen justice.

Administer goodness and you will see an increase in trust.

Give your good example and you will ensure the worthiness of your character.

The resources of creation are distributed by the Creator to his creatures so that they may give continuously and multiply infinitely.

You will be helped by heaven according to how you are helping on the earth.

We have what we give.

Therefore, remember that you are the steward of the life you are living.

Give your neighbors something more than your money. Give them your interest, your health, your joy and your time also, and you will actually find yourself in possession of the sublime gifts of love, balance, happiness and peace, today and tomorrow, in this world and in the life eternal.

~ 118 ~

In Our Endeavors

...do not be ambitious for lofty matters, but associate with the humble. – Paul (Rom. 12:16)

"Do not be ambitious for lofty matters, but associate with the humble," the apostle suggests wisely.

Many disciples of the Gospel long for great accomplishments from one day to the next...

The crown of sanctity...

The power of healing...

The glory of superior knowledge...

Edification of great importance...

However, aspiring by itself is not enough for accomplishment.

Everything in the circles of nature obeys the spirit of sequence.

The victorious tree first started out as a fragile sprout.

The waterfall that moves powerful turbines is a coming together of streams of water.

The plan to build a stately house is majestic, but the pickaxe, shovel, brick and stone are essential so that art and comfort may be expressed.

Let us embrace our humble duties with devotion to our ideal of progress and triumph.

No matter how hard and humble our obligations may be, let us attend to them with love.

Paul's words are wise and right, for if we firmly climb up the lower parts of the mountain, we will easily reach the top, and by willingly accepting the small tasks, great ones will spontaneously come to us.

~ 119 ~

Listen Now

Listen now, you who say... tomorrow...
(Js. 4:13)

Now is the right moment to do the Good.
Tomorrow, probably...
The friend will have left.
The difficulty will be bigger.
The disease will have become worse.
The wound will have opened further.
The problem will be more complicated.
The opportunity to help will not be repeated.
The good seed planted now is a guarantee of the valuable production tomorrow.
The useful word said right now will always be a light in the situation in which you find yourself.
If you wish to be forgiven for any wrong, then approach now those whom you have hurt and show them that you mean to set things right.

If you intend to help your friend, then do it right now so that the blessing of your fraternal assistance may respond to his or her needs with the desired effectiveness.

Do not sleep on the chance to do what is best.

Do not stand around in idle expectation when you can contribute to someone's joy and peace.

A gift too late has the taste of gall.

"Listen now," – says the Gospel in the apostolic word.

Postponing the good we can do is misusing our time and stealing from the Lord.

~ 120 ~

Thus It Will Be

"Thus are those who store up riches for themselves but who are not rich in God." – Jesus. (Lk. 12:21)

You may have countless assets on earth, but if you are not the lord of your own soul, then all of them will be nothing more than a simple introduction to madness.

You may multiply marvelous gardens of youthful joy about you, but if you do not acquire more knowledge for your pathway of tomorrow, your youth will be the noisy eve of true old age.

You may decorate your chest with medals, increasing the number of admirers that applaud you, but if the light of a clear conscience does not bathe your soul, you will be like a coffer of darkness, adorned on the outside but empty on the inside.

You may accumulate wealth and be surrounded by the comfort of your earthly home, and you may dress it in artistic splendors, but if you do not have harmony in your home – which sustains the joy of living – your house will be only a decorated mausoleum.

You may pile up gold and silver coins, in the shadow of which you may speak with authority and influence to those around you, but if your possessions are not spread around in the form of assistance and work, incentive and education on their behalf, you will be only a carefree traveler on the way to terrifying disillusionment.

You may grow horizontally; you may win power and fame; you may be treated with reverence during your physical presence on earth, but if you do not develop values of the Good, you will rub shoulders with the unfortunate on an unforeseen march towards the ruins of disenchantment.

Thus it will be with "all those who stores up treasures for themselves but who are not rich in God."

~ 121 ~

Let Us Seek the Light

All scripture inspired by God is useful ... for instruction in righteousness. — Paul. (2 Tim. 3:16)

Seek an idea according to its value.

When money comes into your hands, you do not ask where it has come from.

You do not know whether it has come from the house of a righteous man or an unrighteous one, or whether, before that, it was used by a saint or a malefactor.

Realizing its importance, you can save it or use it sensibly because you have learned that it bears the stamp of the authority that guides you in the daily struggle.

Money is a representation of the acquisitive power of the temporal government to which you are subject; hence, you do not argue about its origin; you respect and use it, according to the possibilities it represents.

Renewing and edifying ideas arise in the same way.

Why should we expect them to be approved by our family members or personal friends in order for them to produce a wholesome effect within us and around us?

Every consoling and instructive page is a gift from Heaven.

It does not matter if the thoughts contained on it have come from the mind of our earthly parents, our children, our dear friends or our fellow human beings.

What matters is the usefulness it may offer us.

The money you use to buy bread today may have been in the hands of your worst enemy yesterday, but it is still a blessing that ensures your sustenance due to its value.

Consequently, a message – whatever its source may be – that leads us to the Good or to the truth is always valuable and holy in essence because if we use it in our soul and in our daily experience, we may acquire the eternal talents of wisdom and love, for they are a tool of salvation that has come from the infinite mercy of our Heavenly Father.

Let us seek the light wherever it may be, and the darkness will never reach us.

~ 122 ~

Let Us Understand One Another

But above all, ardently love one another. – Peter. (1 Pet. 4:8)

There are no bigger or smaller endeavors. All of them are important.

One person is respected due to the laws he or she passes; another is admired because of his or her deeds. But neither the legislator nor the hero could stand out if not for the humble labor of the farmer who sows the field, or without the anonymous effort of the sweeper who cleans the public streets.

Therefore, do not isolate yourself in the pride with which you think you are better than everyone else.

The community is a team that serves, creating the wealth of experience. And we must not forget that the harmony of that living mechanism depends on us.

When we are able to spread the stimulus of our understanding and collaboration to all, respecting the importance of our own endeavor and the excellence of other people's as well, the earth will be renewed on its road to perfect happiness.

But for that happen, we must reciprocally devote ourselves to one another with ardent, fraternal love…

Let us love our position in the social order no matter how humble or rudimentary it may be, lending our best efforts to the Good, to progress and to education.

We will be understood according to our understanding.

Let us see our neighbor embodied in his or her effort, and our neighbor will see us embodied in our endeavors.

Let us reach out to those around us and they will respond with the best they have.

The most precious capital of life is that of goodwill. Let us use goodwill and our life will be enriched with blessings and joys, today and always, wherever we may be.

~ 123 ~

Living in Peace

...Live in peace... – Paul. (2 Cor. 13:11)

Keep yourself in peace.

Others will probably war against you without reason, criticizing you for the way you live your life; nevertheless, you can continue on your pathway without warring against others.

To do so, however – so that tranquility may bathe your mind – compassion and goodness must follow all your footsteps.

Promise yourself that you will do all you can to avoid exasperation.

If you maintain your serenity, you can analyze every event and every person in their respective place and position.

Notice with a caring attitude all those that come your way...

All those who appear, afflicted or desperate, irascible or violent, bear wounds or illusions. Prisoners of vanity or ignorance, they have not been able to tolerate the light of the truth; consequently, they complain angrily ... Anoint yourself with mercy and enter the recesses of their being, and you see all of them as spiritual children who feel outraged or hurt.

Some accuse; others weep.

Help them while you can.

By pacifying their soul, you will harmonize your own life even more.

Let us learn to understand each mind according to its problem.

Remember that nature, always divine at heart, respects the law of balance and conserves it incessantly.

Even when people are frantic and in open conflict, the earth is always firm and the sun continues to shine.

Living haphazardly is normal for everybody, but living in peace with oneself is the work of a few.

~ 124 ~

Do Not Become Weary

Let us not become weary of doing good, for at the proper time we will reap a harvest if we do not give up. – Paul. (Gal. 6:9)

When the chisel began to smite the block of raw marble, the stone, in despair, complained against its fate. But later, when it saw that it was admired as one of the most beautiful artistic conceptions in the world, it praised the chisel that had broken it apart.

As the caterpillar was moving along with extreme difficulty, it saw the lovely, fragrant flowers and rebelled against its ugly body. One day, however, the viscous body in which it had suffered became an agile, graceful butterfly. Then, it praised the ugly body with which nature had prepared it for happy flight.

When the red-hot iron was put on the anvil, it became frightened and it suffered unwillingly; but when it found itself performing an important function in the machines of progress, it smiled gratefully at the fire that had purified and ennobled it.

When the seed was thrown into the dark hole, it wept and despaired, and asked why it had been abandoned so utterly;

however, when it found itself becoming tall and lush, it moved towards the sun and made itself a respected and benevolent tree, blessing the soil that had isolated it.

Do not weary of doing good.

Those who do not understand your goodwill today will praise your devotion and effort tomorrow.

Never despair; help always.

Perseverance is the foundation for victory.

Do not forget that, in your farming of love and light, you will reap later, but only by going forward amid sweat and confidence, without becoming discouraged, will you achieve the divine harvest.

~ 125 ~

Richly

May the word of Christ dwell in you richly...
– Paul. (Col. 3:16)

You say you trust in the power of Christ, but if the day appears in colors that are contrary to your expectations, you demonstrate a deplorable lack of faith by your rebelliousness.

You say that you are cultivating the love that the Master has bequeathed to us, but if your neighbor has points of view that differ from yours, you show an enormous dearth of understanding by entrusting yourself to dissatisfaction and criticism.

You say that you believe the Gospel in all its simplicity and purity, but if the Lord asks you to make some sacrifice that is perfectly compatible with your capabilities, you demonstrate an uncontestable lack cooperation, issuing challenges and asking for reparations.

You say you try to do the Will of the Heavenly Benefactor, but if your whims are not satisfied, you show a lamentable lack of patience and hope, casting your best thoughts into the swamp of disenchantment.

However, can we ever light a candle if we remain in the dark?

Can we display obedience if we praise rebelliousness?

Can we ever teach serenity if we are inclined towards desperation?

Can we proclaim the glory of love if we cultivate hatred?

The word of Christ does not ask us to progress in weakness or lamentation, as if we were wards of ignorance.

According to Paul's illuminated conceptualization, the Good News should shine forth from our lives, dwelling in our souls richly.

~ 126 ~

Let Us Help Always

"And who is my neighbor?" – (Lk. 10:29)

The neighbor to whom we must render immediate assistance is always the one who is closest to us.

In short, he or she is, in every way, the person who shadows our footsteps. And since the Divine Law recommends that we love our neighbor as ourselves, let us prepare to help, infinitely...

If it is a family member, let us help him or her with our active cooperation.

If it is a hierarchical superior, let us practice respect and goodwill.

If one of our subordinates comes looking for us, let us assist him or her with attention and kindness.

If a malefactor comes to us, let us practice fraternity, trying, without affectation, to open to him or her new pathways to the Good.

If a sick person asks for our help, let us show compassion for his or her situation whatever it may be.

If a good person is helped by our word, let us encourage him or her to make him or herself even better.

If a bad person seeks our influence, let us assist him or her without ostentation so that he or she may rectify him or herself.

If Christianity indwells our conscience, the systematic cultivation of understanding and goodness has the force of law in our lives.

Christians who are not involved in endeavors for the Good are in a bad state of affairs and they weigh heavily on the economy of society.

In the Gospel, remaining neutral means making very little effort.

With Jesus near us, let us act closely with him; if Jesus is far off, we will delay the advance of the light. And we know that the Master loved and assisted; he fought for the light and resisted darkness all the way to the cross.

Therefore, before the neighbor who approaches your heart each day, always remember that you have been placed on this earth to learn and to help.

~ 127 ~

Royal Humanity

"Behold the man!" – Pilate. (Jn. 19:5)

In presenting Christ to the crowd, Pilate did not designate him as an earthly conqueror...
No banquet, no purple.
No applause, no flowers.
Jesus was facing death.
A week of terrible suffering was about to end.
Betrayed, he had not rebelled.
Arrested, he had practiced patience.
Humiliated, he had not retorted.
Forgotten, he had not been indignant.
Derided, he had forgiven.
Whipped, he forgot the offense.
Victimized by injustice, he did not defend himself.
Condemned to martyrdom, he was able to forgive.
Crucified, he would soon return to join the same disciples and beneficiaries that had abandoned him, renewing their hopes.

However, showing him to the people, Pilate did not say, "Behold the criminal," or "Behold the victim!"

He said simply, "Behold the man!"

Apparently defeated, the Master appeared in full spiritual grandeur, revealing the highest standard for human dignity.

Therefore, as we recall this passage, let us remember that only by following the moral lines of Christ will we ever attain Royal Humanity.

~ 128 ~

Do Not Discard Your Confidence

Therefore, do not discard your confidence, which has great reward. – Paul. (Heb. 10:35)

Do not discard the confidence that nourishes your heart.

Very often, the apparent progress of the impious discourages the fervor of tepid souls.

Faltering virtue retreats before seemingly victorious vice.

The fragile believer is pained before the wrongdoer who is heaped with praise.

Nevertheless, if we have accepted Jesus as our Divine Master, we must receive the world as our educational institution.

And this school shows us that the physical journey is but a training period for the spirit in the immense field of life.

Every century has had its dominating sovereigns.

Many of them set themselves up on pedestals of gold and power at the expense of the blood and tears of their contemporaries.

Many won battles of hatred.
Others monopolized bread.
Some controlled political life.
Others earned the people's fear.

Nonetheless, all of them died ... As an earthly prize for the laborious endeavors to which they devoted themselves, they received only an opulent tomb, where they underscore the cold house of death.

Do not discard your faith because your educational experience on earth imposes on your vision afflictive circumstances in the game of human conventions.

Remember immortality – our divine inheritance!

Wherever you go, conduct your soul as a precious source of comprehension and service! Wherever you are, be generous, optimistic and diligent in doing the Good!

The flesh is only your clothing.

Struggle and become a better person. Work and accomplish with Christ. Wait confidently for the future, with the certainty that life awaits you today, and it will always be fair and just tomorrow.

~ 129 ~

Be Patient

You need patience so that after you have done God's Will you may receive the promise. — Paul. (Heb. 10:36)

You have probably been holding on to tormented hope for a long time.

You would like the world's answer to your longings to appear immediately, enfolding your heart; however, what kind of peace could you enjoy in the apparent triumph of your dreams if you have not redeemed the debts that chain you to problems and difficulties?

How can you have a moment's rest, when your creditor is demanding payment?

Could a criminal find rest in light of the due reparation for the crime he or she has committed?

You know that destiny will materialize your plans for happiness, that victory will finally crown your pathway of struggle, but you find yourself bound to the circle of certain obligations:

Your home, which has become a forge of anguish...

Your workplace, where you suffer slander or cruelty...

The family member to whom you owe respect and love, but from whom you receive scorn and ingratitude...

The web of obstacles...

The conspiracy of the darkness...

Needless persecution; the infirmity of the body; the impositions of your environment...

If trials have imprisoned you behind the restraining bars of a duty you have to fulfill, be patient and satisfy the obligations you have embraced!

Do not renounce your renewing endeavor!

Remember that God's Will is expressed each hour in the circumstances that surround us! Let us pay our debts to the darkness so that the Light may bless us!

Yes, we will accomplish the materialization of our plans for happiness, but before that, we must patiently liquidate the debts we have contracted before the Law.

~ 130 ~

In the Inner Sphere

Let each one of us serve others with the gift we have received, as good stewards of the multiform grace of God. – Peter. (1 Pet. 4:10)

Life is a divine machine, of which all beings are important parts, and cooperation is the essential factor for producing harmony and the goodness for everyone.

There is nothing that does not have meaning.

No one is useless.

Each person has received a certain talent from Divine Providence in order to serve the world and receive from the world the wages of spiritual growth.

Old or young, healthy in body or not, remember that you are to use the gift you have received from the Lord so that you may advance towards the Great Light.

None are so poor that they cannot give of themselves.

Even paralytics bound to the cot of infirmity can furnish calmness and patience to others by expressing peace and resignation.

So, do not neglect the work that Heaven has entrusted to you, and avoid the preoccupation of interfering in your neighbor's task under the pretext of helping.

Those who fulfill their duties act naturally on behalf of the overall equilibrium.

Many times, believing we can do other people's work better than they can, we are nothing but agents of disharmony and trouble.

Wherever we are, let us use diligence and nobility to accomplish the mission that life offers us.

Remember that time is the same for everyone, and that it is our silent and inflexible judge.

Yesterday, today and tomorrow are three phases of the single pathway.

Every day is an opportunity to sow and reap.

Therefore, let us do our job and remember the words of the Gospel: "Let each one of us serve others with the gift we have received, as good stewards of the multiform grace of God," so that God's grace may enrich us with new blessings.

~ 131 ~

In the Social Arena

But he said to them, "You give them something to eat." – (Mk. 6:37)

Faced with the weary, hungry multitude, Jesus told his disciples: "You give them something to eat."

The Master's remark is very important because he could have told them to scold the crowd for being imprudent for having made such an exhaustive trip to the mount without bringing something to eat.

But the Master wanted to engrave on his disciples' minds their dedication to serving people. He taught that, in view of the needy crowd, servants of the Gospel have only one duty: rendering disinterested and fraternal assistance.

At the time of that unforgettable teaching, hunger was something natural for the weary body, but as usual, we see the multitude lacking assistance, dominated by the hunger for light and harmony, and flogged by the invisible lashes of discord and incomprehension.

Jesus' coworkers are not called to sadden the people with pessimism, disturb them with disorder or to immobilize them with discouragement. Instead, they are called to feed them with enlightenment and peace, moral strength and sublime hope.

If you find yourself around people whom you want to help, and if you want to contribute to the regeneration of the social arena, then do not waste your time on preaching rebelliousness and despair. Maintain your peace-of-mind and feed your neighbor with your good example and your good word.

Remember the Lord's order: "You give them something to eat."

~ 132 ~

Being Afraid

"I was afraid, so I hid your talent in the ground..." – (Mt. 25:25)

In the parable of talents, the negligent servant attributes his unhappy failure to fear.

He had received less potential to realize a profit.

He had only one talent accounted to him and he was afraid of struggling to make it grow.

Similar to what happened to the careless servant in the gospel narrative, there are many people who blame their meager resources for not being able to do what they want. So, they remain idle and say they are afraid to do anything.

Afraid of working.

Afraid of serving.

Afraid of making friends.

Afraid of being a disappointment.

Afraid of suffering.

Afraid of being misunderstood.

Afraid of happiness.

Afraid of suffering.

They reach the end of their physical body as human sensitives, without having made the least effort to enrich their lives.

In life, they fear death.

In death, they fear life.

And under the pretext of being disfavored by fate, they gradually become champions of uselessness and idleness.

So, if you have received a harder task in the world, do not be afraid. Make it your way of progress and renewal. No matter how dark the road to which circumstances have led you, enrich it with the light of your effort at doing the Good, because being afraid was not an acceptable excuse in settling accounts between servant and master.

~ 133 ~

What Do You Have?

"How many loaves do you have?" And they said to him, "Seven." – (Mk. 8:5)

When faced with the hungry multitude, Jesus asked his disciples if there was any way they might be able to feed them. He was obviously looking for something that would serve as a basis for materializing the help they needed.

"How many loaves do you have?"

This question shows the need for some kind of concourse in the work of multiplication.

Mark the Evangelist tells us that Jesus' disciples presented him with seven small loaves, which more than 4,000 people were able to feed on and from which there were even leftovers.

Would the Master have managed such a feat if he had not been able to count on some resource?

This image compels us to think about how important our cooperation is so that the Heavenly Benefactor may enrich us with his gifts of abundant life.

Can the Christ build the sanctuary of happiness within us and for us if he cannot count on the bases of the goodwill in our hearts?

The most powerful electric plant still needs a humble outlet to light a room.

Many people hope for a miracle from the Lord to satiate their hunger for peace and comfort, but the Master's voice on the mount still resounds, unforgettable:

"What do you have?"

God's goodness is infinite; still, something must emerge from our "self" on our behalf.

In any arena of our accomplishments for the higher life, let us offer Jesus as least a few scraps of personal effort; then we can be sure that the Lord will do the rest.

~ 134 ~

Let Us Seek Balance

Those who claim to abide in him must also live as he did. – John. (1 Jn. 2:6)

Although you should walk without fear, do not be imprudent under the pretext of cultivating fearlessness.

If we devote ourselves to the Gospel, let us seek to act according to the Divine Master's standards, which never give way to temerity.

Jesus emphasizes the imperative of building the Kingdom of God, but he does not sacrifice other people's interests by rushing the work.

He advises the sincerity of "yes, yes – no, no," but that does not mean being rude about it.

He points out the moral ruins of dogmatic Pharisaism, but he still reveres the Law of Moses.

He calls Lazarus from the tomb, but he does not nourish the pretension of exempting him completely from the death of the body.

Aware of the power with which he has been vested, he does not despise political authority, which should govern according to the necessities of the people, and he teaches that one should "render unto Caesar what is Caesar's and to God what is God's."

Arrested and condemned to death, he does not waste time on boasting, in spite of knowing the devotion with which he is followed by angelic entities.

Let us heed the Divine Model. Let us remember it by fulfilling our duty with faithfulness and courage. But let us avoid unnecessary bravery, which is the same as dangerous frivolity.

A fearful heart paralyzes one's ability to work.

A reckless heart sets fire to any endeavor and destroys it.

Therefore, let us seek Jesus-centered balance and we will naturally avoid extremism, which is always a dark sign of disharmony or violence, of disturbance or death.

~ 135 ~

Forgive Always

"If you forgive other people's offenses, your Heavenly Father will forgive yours." – Jesus. (Mt. 6:14)

No matter how serious your neighbor's wrongs may seem to be, do not waste your time on criticism.

Condemning strengthens the darkness and sets up barriers to serving the light.

Regarding victims of evil, look for some good with which you may uplift them, just as life performs the miracle of making apparently dead trees green again.

Before anything else, remember how difficult it is to judge people's decisions concerning experiences that are different from our own!

How can we reflect if we appropriate someone else's conscience, and how can we sense reality if we use a heart that does not belong to us?

If the world around you cries out in alarm today, remain silent and wait…

An appropriate remark is impracticable when fog surrounds us.

Tomorrow, when your equilibrium is restored, you will have enough light so that the darkness does not alter your understanding.

Moreover, with regard to problems involving criticism, do not think you are beyond criticism yourself.

Due to noxious self-complacency, you do not notice how often you seem unkind towards others!

If there are those who love our praiseworthy qualities, there are also those who point out our faults and defects.

If there are those who help us, praising our luminous future, there are also those who trouble us, forcing us to review the dark past.

Therefore, practice goodness and forgive always.

The Good News teaches us that Love covers a multitude of sins.

Those who forgive, forgetting evil and living the Good, receive from the Heavenly Father, in the sympathy and cooperation of their neighbor, the charter of self-liberation, making them capable of sublime renewals.

~ 136 ~

Let Us Live Peaceably

May you seek to live quietly. – Paul. (1 Thess. 4:11)

Living quietly does not mean rotting away in idleness.

There are people whose physical body lies supine, shielded against the cold of difficulty by excellent bedcovers of economic ease, but they are tormented mentally by indefinable afflictions.

Living calmly, therefore, does not mean sleeping in stagnation.

Peace derives from having a debt-free conscience, and labor lies at the base of such balance.

If we want health, we have to struggle for the harmony of the body.

If we expect an abundant harvest, we have to sow with effort and defend the crop with perseverance and care.

In order to strengthen our heart against the assault of evil, we must know how to live serenely, working faithfully on our commitments to order and to the Good.

The progress of the impious and the repose of the morally delinquent are stopovers at the entrance to the hell they are creating for themselves.

So, do not strive to be quiet without effort, struggle, toil, problems...

In keeping with the apostle's advice, however, let us leave peaceably, fulfilling, with courage, goodwill and a spirit of sacrifice, the edifying duties the world imposes on us each day for our own good.

~ 137 ~

Let Us Attend To the Good

"In truth I say to you that as often as you did it to one of the least of these my brothers, you did to me." – Jesus. (Mt. 25:40)

Not only with words, which are like glistening leaves on a fruitless branch.

Not only with the act of believing, which is often nothing but idle ecstasy.

Not only with authority, which on many occasions can lead to abuse.

Not only with affirmations of faith, because in many cases, sonorous utterances are the cries of an empty soul.

Let us not forget "doing."

Our connection with Christ, our communion with the Divine Light, does not depend on how we interpret revelations from Heaven.

In every circumstance of his ministry of love, Jesus sought to call people's attention not to the form of religious thought, but to human goodness.

The Good News does not promise the peace of the higher life to those who scrape their knees from making incomprehensible penances; to those who speculate on the nature of God; to those who argue about the things of heaven; or to those who merely preach the eternal truths. It exalts the sublime position of all those who disseminate love in the name of the All-Merciful.

Jesus does not compromise himself with those who make war in his name; with those who humiliate others under the pretext of glorifying him, or with those who offered him opulent worship in churches made of stone and gold. Rather, he says that the smallest gesture of goodness done in his name will always be seen in heaven as an offering of love addressed to him.

~ 138 ~

The Right Remedy

Now we do not need to write to you concerning fraternal charity, for you yourselves have been taught by God that you are to love one another. – Paul. (1 Thess. 4:9)

In its mission as Consoler, Spiritism receives hundreds of thousands of requests from anxious souls who beg for help in solving various problems.

Here, a father who lacks understanding and who uses cruel means to educate his children.

There, a rebellious and ungrateful son who flees the beauty of comprehension.

Over there, someone who is fascinated by the appearances of the world, and who abandons his commitments to a higher ideal.

Yonder, a brother who refuses to offer fraternal help.

In another place, a wife who deserts her home.

Somewhere else, an unfeeling, unreasonable boss.

Nevertheless, for centuries, the remedy for extinguishing these old enigmas involving human relationships has been pointed out in the teachings of the Good News.

Fraternal charity is the key to all the doors to good understanding.

The disciple of the Gospel is someone who has been admitted into the presence of the Divine Master in order to serve.

And the reward for such a worker cannot be expected in the immediacy of earthly society.

How can one put fruit on the green shoot of a newborn tree?

How can one bring forth a masterpiece from the block of marble with only the first strike of the chisel?

Those who truly love in Jesus' name are sowing to reap a harvest in Eternity.

Let us not look for other people's guidance concerning issues that are obviously solvable by our own efforts.

We know that desperation or cursing does no good...

Each spirit has its own pathway to follow.

Therefore, in the light of fraternal charity, let us walk the pathway that life has given us, today and always.

~ 139 ~

Concerning the Work of Salvation

For God did not appoint us to suffer wrath, but to receive salvation through our Lord Jesus Christ. – Paul. (1 Thess. 5:9)

Why are we not understood?

What is the reason for the loneliness that invades our lives?

What are the reasons for the problems that surround us?

Why so much darkness and bitterness surrounding our footsteps?

And each such question we ask ourselves is usually followed by desperation and rebelliousness, and under lethal waves of anger we claim favors that we think are owed to us.

We say we are disappointed in our family, forsaken by our friends, misunderstood by our colleagues, and even persecuted by our brothers and sisters.

Mental intemperance brings to our innermost being the thorns of disenchantment and perilous organic imbalances, turning our lives into a rosary of lazy, sickly complaints.

This happens, however, because the Lord has not appointed us to the dark precipice of wrath, but to the work of salvation.

No one can work in the darkness of disorder.

No one can help by continuously harming others for the sheer pleasure of harming.

No one can bless one's daily chores by cursing them at the same time.

No one can be both a friend and a tormenter.

If you have received notice of the Gospel in the world of your soul, then prepare yourself to help infinitely…

Earth is our school and our workshop.

Humankind is our family.

Each day is a blessed opportunity to learn and to help.

No matter how bad your situation may be, always strive to be helpful and supportive, and you will be involved in the blessed work of salvation to which the Lord has called us.

~ 140 ~

Behind Jesus

And as they were leading him away, they seized one Simon, a Cyrene, who had come in from the country, and they put the cross on his shoulder so as to carry it behind Jesus. – (Lk. 23:26)

The crowd that surrounded the Master on his final day was huge.

It included the impenitent idlers of the world, the champions of usury, the mockers, the ignorant, the weak minds that recognized Christ's superiority and were afraid to stand up for their convictions; the wavering friends of the Gospel, the cowardly witnesses, the beneficiaries of the Divine Physician, who hid themselves in fear, afraid of death ...

But a foreigner, forced by the people, accepted the cross, although constrainedly, and carried it, following behind Jesus.

The lesson, however, would be bequeathed to the centuries of the future...

The world is still an enormous Jerusalem, congregating people of the widest variety of nuances, but if you draw near to the Gospel with sincerity and fervor, they will lay the cross on your heart.

From then on, you will be compelled to make major demonstrations of selflessness; very few will notice your exhaustion and anguish; and in spite of your status as a servant who has the same problems as everyone else, they will expect from you displays of humility, endurance, heroism and loyalty to the Good.

Endure and toil, your eyes turned towards the Divine Light.

Invisible torrents from heavenly springs will descend from On High upon your spirit, and you shall overcome, valiantly.

For now, the cross is still the sign of faithful disciples.

If you do not bear witness through the marks of responsibility, toil, sacrifice, or spiritual growth, it may be that you do love the Master deeply, but it is almost certain that you still have not joined him on the redemptive journey.

Therefore, let us bless our cross and fearlessly follow behind him, seeking the victory of love and eternal resurrection.

~ 141 ~

Renew Yourself Always

Even though our outward man is wasting away, our inner man is being renewed day by day. — Paul. (2 Cor. 4:16)

Each day has a lesson for us.
Each experience leaves behind its corresponding value.
Each problem entails a determined objective.
There are those who, tormented by counterproductive fears, express their rebelliousness when faced with infirmity, poverty, disillusionment or old age.
In the scene of the daily struggle, there is no lack of those who spectacularly flee their responsibilities, seeking, in their discontinuance of the good fight and in their gradual agreement with death, peace, which they cannot find.
Remember that civilizations have come and gone for thousands of years, and that human beings, no matter how happy and powerful they might be, have had to lose their vehicle of flesh to settle their moral accounts with eternity.

Even when the trial seems invincible, or when pain shows itself insuperable, do not withdraw yourself from the position of fighter, in which Divine Providence has placed you.

Remember that, tomorrow, the day will return to your arena of work.

Stand firm in your area of service, teaching your mind to accept God's will.

Sickness may only be a temporary and healthy summons handed down by Heavenly Justice.

A scarcity of earthly resources is always an educational obstacle.

A disappointment received with fervent courage is a work of the Lord's choosing on our behalf.

The aging of the physical body is the solidification of wisdom for eternal happiness.

Be optimist and diligent in the Good amidst confidence and joy, for while the envelope of flesh gradually wastes away, the imperishable soul renews itself, moment by moment for life everlasting.

~ 142 ~

Do Not Steal

Those who have been stealing must steal no longer; instead, they should work, doing something useful with their hands so that they may have something to share with those in need.
– Paul. (Eph. 4:28)

There are ways to steal that have never been cataloged in the codes of earthly justice.

Stealing time from those who work.

Assailing the peace-of-mind of one's neighbor.

Breaking someone else's trust.

Invading other people's interests.

Using thought for undue appropriations.

Plundering other people's joys and hopes.

Using the wrongful keys of intrigue, slander, cruelty and disloyalty, there are ruthless souls that subtly enter unsuspecting hearts, robbing them of their most valuable spiritual treasures…

That is why Paul's words are clothed in sublime meaning: "Those who have been stealing must steal no longer."

If you have accepted the Gospel as the high standard of your life, then above all, seek to use your hands on spiritually constructive activities so that you may be truly useful to those in need.

Evil resides in idleness.

Those who do something have something to share.

Go to your workstation and worthily fulfill your obligations each day, and minding those that the Lord has entrusted to you, you will go down life's road without stealing from anyone.

~ 143 ~

Wake Up and Help

"Follow me, and let the dead take care of burying their dead." – Jesus. (Mt. 8:22)

Jesus did not tell the would-be follower to let the "corpses take care of burying their corpses"; he said: let the "dead take care of burying their dead."

In reality, there is a big difference.

A corpse is lifeless flesh, whereas a dead person is someone who withdraws from life.

There are many people who walk in the shadows of death without being dead.

They are deserters of evolution; they shut themselves up between the walls of their own mind and remain attached to selfishness and vanity, refusing to share their life experience with others.

They immerse themselves in graves of gold, of vice, of bitterness and illusion. If they are victimized by the temptation of riches, they dwell in graves of money; if they are defeated by pernicious habits, they imprison themselves in jails of darkness;

if they are prostrated by discouragement, they sleep in tears of moral bankruptcy, and if they are tormented by their own lies, they live under tombstones of deadly deceit.

Learn to participate in the collective struggle.

Each day, get out of yourself and try to feel your neighbor's suffering, the need of those close to you, the distress of your brothers and sisters, and help as much as you can.

Do not confine yourself in the sphere of your "self."

Awaken and live with everyone, to everyone and for everyone, for no one lives only to oneself.

In any part of the world, we are beneficiaries of the effort and sacrifice of thousands of lives.

Let us give something of ourselves on behalf of others in exchange for the much that others are doing for us.

In this way, let us remember the teaching of Christ.

Regarding your works of charity, if you find a corpse, give it the blessing of a grave; but regarding the spiritual journey, always let "the dead take care of burying their dead."

~ 144 ~

Let Us Assist the Mental Life

And he was followed by a large crowd from Galilee, the Decapolis, Jerusalem, Judea and from beyond the Jordan. – (Mt. 4:25)

The multitudes continue to follow Jesus in the hopes of meeting him, and they use all the means within their reach to do so.

They come from everywhere, eager for comfort and revelation.

The interference of all who try to stand between the multitude and the Lord is futile because, century after century, the search and hope have intensified.

Therefore, in our condition as disciples, let us remember that any assistance we may be able to lend to people will always be blessed.

One does not have to be a statesperson or an administrator to assist them in order to grow spiritually.

Goodwill and cooperation are the two master columns in the edifice of human fraternity, and contributing so that society may learn to think about spreading the Good means cooperating so that the earthly mind may be put in harmony with the Divine Mind.

An invaluable plan has been revealed to us in this regard: Education.

Spiritually constructive reading.

Instructive lectures.

A contagious example in the practice of simple goodness.

The dissemination of consoling and instructive books.

The practice of meditation.

May our primary endeavor be the awakening of inner, personal qualities.

Let us help others do all they can to improve social progress in their own sphere and activity.

To guide the thought, to enlighten and sublimate it is to guarantee the redemption of the world, unveiling rich, new horizons for ourselves.

Let us assist the mental life of the multitude, and we will all meet Jesus more easily for the victory of Life Eternal.

145

Beware of the Dogs

Beware of the dogs. – Paul. (Phil. 3:2)

We are a long caravan of beings on the evolutionary road, moving about under the eyes of the Divine Shepherd on our way to higher realms.

In fact, as we proceed on our journey, magnetized by the devotion of our Divine Leader, we are inevitably besieged by the dogs of ignorance, perversity and disloyalty.

When he referred to dogs, Paul of Tarsus did not have in mind the animal friend, a symbol of love and faithfulness after having been domesticated. He was referring to wild, impulsive, ferocious dogs. Within the human flock, there are always people who personify them. They are the systematic enemies of the Good.

They destroy worthy reputations.

They love slander.

They practice cruelty.

They feel pleasure at imposing their tyranny on others.

They undo the lofty, sanctified meaning of life.

They undermine the work of well-intentioned souls.

They ruthlessly infiltrate constructive endeavors in order to destroy and pervert them.

They spew insults and slander.

In their thoughtlessness, they cry out that evil is victorious, that the darkness has triumphed, that misery has consolidated its dominion on the earth, thus wreaking havoc on the peace of industrious, faithful workers.

And whenever the microbe of hatred or anger excites their desperation, woe to those who approach them with benevolence and trust!

It is this type of brothers and sisters that Paul asks us to apply the verb "beware." For them, poor prisoners of incomprehension and ignorance, only the educational process remains, in which we may cooperate with love. However, we need to realize that this means of domestication proceeds first from God.

~ 146 ~

Let Us Work Together

"For without me you can do nothing." – Jesus. (Jn. 15:5)

The divine power of Christ, as God's representative, lies latent in all people. Every man and woman has received a sacred gift from him, even though many of them are outside of religious circles.

However, we are here referring to those who cultivate their faith, those who have begun the long, laborious effort of discovering the sublime values that vibrate within them.

Many of them yearn for spectacular demonstrations by Jesus on their pathway, and countless learners believe that only those involved in preaching from the pulpits of the various religious confessions are working with the Lord.

It is crucial to correct this interpretative error, however.

The Lord is with us in every situation of life. We can do nothing without the influx of his sovereign will.

The Master tells us clearly: "I am the vine; you are the branches." How can anything be produced without the essential sap?

Actually, founded on the same bases, astute learners may object, saying that there are also those who practice evil according to this criterion. In response, let us just remember that such unfortunate people, on their own account, have grafted infernal cacti onto the Divine Vine and they will pay a high price before the Governor of the Universe.

We are referring to timid and wavering, although well-intentioned individuals, and can conclude that, in all human endeavors, we can feel the presence of the Lord sanctifying the work that has been committed to us. Thus, let us remember the evangelical teaching that says that any effort for the Good will be blessed, even if it involves only giving a glass of pure water in his name.

The Master is not only to be found in the work of those who teach the Divine Revelation through the academic, instructive or consoling word. He accompanies those who manage the world's assets and those who obey the demands of the way by contributing to building a better tomorrow both in physical and spiritual organizations. He stands alongside those who till the soil of the Planet, collaborating in constructing a Perfected Earth, thus following the missionaries of intelligence in the evolution of human rights.

In this way, let us work together in the area to which we have been called for Christian service.

Do the best you can in the bit of the endeavor that has been entrusted into your hands.

Today, perhaps you are mistaken if you think you are serving earthly authorities. The revealing moment will come when you realize that you are actually serving the Lord. So, join the Divine Artisan in spirit and truth, because the fundamental issue of our peace-of-mind lies in knowing if we are living in him as much as he is living in us.

~ 147 ~

Seek Refuge in Peace

There were so many who were coming and going that they did not even have time to eat.
– (Mk. 6:31)

The Master's invitation to his disciples to seek an isolated place in order to rest their minds and hearts in prayer is becoming more and more appropriate.

Earth's roads are filled with those who are coming and going, tormented by immediate interests but finding no time to receive spiritual nourishment. Countless people travel the pathway in their hunger for wealth, only to return overwhelmed in disillusionment. Many others seek adventures, eager for excitement, only to return inflicted with destructive boredom.

Never have there been as many stone places of worship for manifestations of religiosity in the world as there are at present, and yet never have souls experienced so much disenchantment.

Labor laws are reducing working hours as never before; but even so, in no other time have there been such anguishing concerns as nowadays.

The machines of modern civilization have amazingly decreased human effort; however, unrest is presently culminating in wars of scientific destruction.

Techniques of economic production have advanced in every area, engineering cotton and wheat in order to increase harvests, but for eyes that contemplate the world landscape there has never been such a dearth of bread and clothing amongst incarnates.

Social theories of solidarity have improved, but there has never been so much discord.

Just as was the case in the times of Jesus' ministry, the majority of men and women are stuck in their comings and goings between a misguided searching and a false finding, of a careless youth and a disillusioned old age, of a neglected health and pointless disease, of a wasted incarnation and a despairing discarnation.

O my friend, if you truly want to learn from the Divine Master, go to an isolated place and cultivate the interests of your soul.

You might not find a garden area that facilitates meditation, or even some bit of physical nature where you may rest from material weariness; even so, you can enter your inner sanctuary.

There are many sentiments within you that have stimulated you for centuries, imitating the comings and goings of the multitude. These sentiments rush from your heart to your brain and from you brain back to your heart, always the same sentiments, incapable of accessing the light of the spirit. These are the imagined principles of peace, justice, love and happiness that the realm of the flesh impose on you. They may even be useful under certain circumstances of the transitory experiences; however, do not live exclusively alongside them. They would exert a hellish captivity over you.

Seek refuge in that isolated temple within your soul, for only there will you find true notions of the peace, justice, love and happiness for which the Lord has destined you.

~ 148 ~

The Father's Heir

...whom he made heir of all things, and through whom he made the world. – Paul. (Heb. 1:2)

Give to respectable human powers what is owing them by logical right of life, but do not forget to give to the Lord what belongs to him.

This conciliatory Gospel formula is still of great interest for the world's well-being.

It is not advisable to concentrate all our hopes and aspirations on the changeable organizations of the corporeal realm.

The inner being renews itself daily. Consequently, the knowledge that meets its demands in the present is not the same that used to help it in the past, and in the future, it will be much different from that of today. The politics of the past has given way to the politics of modern struggles. The bloody triumph of the strongest in times of ruthless savagery was followed by militarist autocracy. Might gave way to authority; authority gave way to right. And in the area of religious activities, such evolutionary effort has been no less obvious.

In view of such realities, why are you so vehemently passionate for fallible people and transitory plans?

The men and women of today, no matter how venerable they may be, are heirs of those of yesterday, employed in the gigantic struggle for self-redemption. They might promise marvelous kingdoms of abundance, peace, freedom and harmony, but they cannot escape the work of correcting the wrongs they have inherited, not only from those who came before them in the area of social commitments, but also from their own past lives due to awful diversions of their sentiments.

Today's civilization is successor to the ones that failed.

Nations that rebuild themselves take advantage of those that unmade themselves.

The organizations that appear today have retained the inheritance of those that vanished in the vortex of discord and tyranny.

Examining the undisguised face of the truth, how are you to hypertrophy your sentiments, defining yourself completely by earthly institutions, which can offer you no spiritual help?

How can a house without a roof shelter you from the storm? The blueprints for a skyscraper, intelligently drawn on parchment, are not yet an actual building.

Therefore, there are no reasons that justify the torments of Christ's followers, who may be anxious about the passing political troubles of today. Such a state of the soul is merely the product of dangerous negligence because we all should know that fallible human beings cannot build infallible works, and that it is up to us, followers of the Master, to act as sincere workers who have been called to serve and cooperate in the long and patient, but permanent and eternal endeavor of the one whom the Father "made heir of all things, and through whom he made the world."

~ 149 ~

The Adoration of Prayer

After they finished praying, the place where they were gathered shook, and they were all filled with the Holy Spirit. – (Acts 4:31)

We all send out creative or destructive energies all around us, and they are either pleasant or unpleasant to our personal circle of activity.

A tree can affect us with the subtle matter of its emanations.

A spider lives in the center of its own web.

A bee may travel far but it does not rest, except in the compartments of its own hive.

In the same way, a person dwells amidst his or her own mental creations.

Our thoughts are either walls in which we imprison ourselves or wings with which we progress on an ascent.

As you think, so shall you live.

Our inner life – our place.

So that we do not disturb the laws of universe, nature only gives us the blessings of life according to our concepts of it.

Confine yourself and you will discover the limit of everything around you.

Expand your horizons and you will find the infinite of everything that exists.

So that we may elevate ourselves using all the elements within our personal orbit, we know of no other means except prayer, which asks for light, love and truth.

Prayer, translating an ardent aspiration to spiritual growth through knowledge and virtue, is a power that illuminates one's ideals and sanctifies one's work.

This passage from Acts says that after the apostles prayed, the place where they were gathered shook and they were filled with the Holy Spirit: their longing for fraternity was illuminated; their minds were enriched with superior purposes and sanctifying power gladdened their spirits.

Therefore, remember that the adoration of prayer is a decisive pathway. Day after day, prayer will renew you for the work of the Lord without your even noticing it.

~ 150 ~

The Prayer of a Righteous Person

The prayer of a righteous person can accomplish much. – (James 5:16)

Considering the vital power contained in waves of desire, every impulse and every longing also comprises a prayer that emanates from nature.

The worm that moves along with difficulty is actually beseeching an easier way to get around.

The she-wolf caressing its cub is imploring lessons of love that may change its savage ways.

Deep in their souls, primitive humans, when worshiping the thunder, are praying for explanations from the Divinity so as to educate their impulses of faith.

All the needs of the world, when translated into the efforts of living beings, are creatures' pleas to the Creator and Father.

For that very reason, if the desire of a good person is a prayer, the purpose of a bad or imbalanced one is also a prayer.

Even then, however, we have the law of specific density.

If you throw a stone at someone, it will immediately start to fall.

If you put a few drops of cologne on someone's forehead, the aroma will spread into the atmosphere.

If you free a snake, it will look for a hole.

If you let the swallow loose, it will fly to the heights.

Minerals, plants, animals and human souls are constantly asking for something, and Divine Providence, through nature, is always answering.

There are solutions that take a long time and answers that take centuries to come down from heaven to earth.

But of all the prayers that do reach heaven, the apostle points out the fact that the prayer of a righteous person is clothed with intense power.

This is because a righteous conscience adjusted to the Law has already earned friendships and innumerable intercessions.

Those who win friends accumulate love. Those who accumulate love, build up power.

So, learn to act with justice and goodness and your prayers will ascend without obstacles, supported by the vehicles of kindness and gratitude because the righteous person, wherever he or she may be, is always a coworker of God.

~ 151 ~

Slander

Brothers, do not speak ill of one another. Anyone who speaks ill of a brother speaks ill of the law and judges the law; and if you judge the law, you are no longer a follower of the law, but a judge. – (Js. 4:11)

Kindness is not always appropriate in the circle of loyal conversations.

Sometimes, a clarifying discussion requires serene yet decided forcefulness; nevertheless, great care in regard to comments made afterwards is indispensable.

Slander lies in wait for sincerity in order to muddy its waters and neutralize its efforts.

Malice does not deserve the crown of serious discussion. Giving it too much importance in conversations actually enlarges its sphere of action. That is why James' advice is clothed in sanctifying wisdom.

When a problem that is hard to solve emerges between two believers, it is best to seek the Master's company and solve it in his clarifying light. They should never give in to the darkness and alienate each other with malicious remarks about the matter, thus increasing the pain of an open wound.

The actual meaning of "to speak ill of," is to render homage to the inferior instincts and to renounce the title of God's coworker to become a critic of his works.

As we can see, slander is a subtle poison that may get the learner in big trouble.

Those who take such poison are, above all, a servant of foolishness, and we know that many such foolish individuals are but one step from awful, inner misfortunes.

~ 152 ~

Come

And let him who hears say, "Come!" Whoever is thirsty, let him come. – (Rev. 22:17)

Earth is the great school of souls where students of all ages are educated.

If you have reached the level of great experiences, do not worry about your ever-increasing workload.

Do not see enemies in those whose understanding is still imperfect. Many of them have not yet left spiritual kindergarten.

Always render good for evil, truth for lie, and love for indifference…

The inexperience and ignorance of souls that have just begun the struggle are often very troubling to the spirit that is in search of itself.

Consequently, you often may suffer from affliction and discouragement.

Do not be troubled, however.

If the illusions and toys of the majority do not satisfy you anymore, it is because maturity is pointing you towards vaster horizons.

Remember that only Jesus is wise and strong enough to bring you peace-of-mind.

Listen to his divine appeal, spoken in the last words of his Testament of Love: "Come!"

Nobody can keep you from approaching the spring of infinite light.

The Master is the Eternal Friend who breaks our chains and opens the doors of renewal…

However, you have to be willing.

The Lord never forces anything on us.

Do you suffer? Are you fatigued? Do you stumble under the burdens of the world?

Come!

Jesus is holding out his arms to you.

Come and meet him yet today. It is true that you have always yearned to serve; that the Master has always been selfless and merciful towards you, but do not forget that circumstances may change with the times and that not all days are the same.

~ 153 ~

Let Us Heed

And immediately he called them. –
(Mk. 1:20)

In some circles of Christianity, this passage, referring to the Lord calling the disciples, is simply understood as a call by Christ to the religious ministry.

However, we may give to it a broader meaning.

In each situation on the way, it is possible to hear the heavenly call.

In the home, where difficult problems may arise...

Before an unknown friend who asks for help...

When facing an adversary who expects understanding and tolerance...

Beside the bed of a sick person who needs assistance and care...

In the presence of an unlearned person who needs help and instruction...

Before a child in need of kindness and understanding...

Wherever we go, Jesus, the Silent Master, calls us to bear witness to the lesson we have learned.

In the smallest experiences, such as at work or play, in the home or out on the street, he is there, inviting us to constantly practice the Good.

In this way, disciples of the Gospel finds this world to be a sanctuary for their faith, and humankind to be their own family.

Thus, by pointing to the Christian norm as inspiration for all our daily chores, let us heed the word of the Lord at every point of the way, seeking to follow him with unwavering faithfulness, today and always.

~ 154 ~

No One Lives solely for Himself

For none of us lives solely for himself... – Paul. (Rom. 14:7)

The tree that you plant will produce not only for your own hunger but for the necessities of others.

The torch you light will illuminate not only the pathway at your own feet but also the path for those with you.

Just like the small stream of water influences the soil over which it passes, your decisions inspire other people's decisions.

Thousands of eyes watch your footsteps; thousands listen to your voice, and thousands of hearts receive your encouragement to do good or evil.

"Nobody lives solely for himself..." says the Divine Message.

Whether we like it or not, the Law demands that our lives be connected to the lives of those around us.

We live for our families, our friends, our ideals...

Even reclusive misers, who think they need no one, live for their gold or for their possessions, which they will have to hand over to other lives when death takes them.

Being aware of such a reality, keep an eye on your own pathway.

When feeling, you think.

When thinking, you do.

And everything that is part of your endeavors, through your intentions, words and actions, will represent the influence of your soul, helping to liberate you for the glory of the light, or worsening your captivity for suffering in the darkness.

So, keep an eye on your inner world and do as much good as you can while it is still today, for according to the wise concept of the Apostle Paul, "Nobody lives solely for himself."

~ 155 ~

Let Us Learn To Give Thanks

Give thanks in everything. –
Paul (1 Thess. 5:18)

Let us know how to give thanks for the gifts the Lord gives us each day:
the fullness of life;
the abundant air;
the blessing of locomotion;
the faculty of reason;
the spark of ideas;
the joy of seeing;
the pleasure of hearing;
the treasure of speaking;
the privilege of working,
the gift of learning,
the table that serves us;
the bread that feeds us;

the cloth that clothes us;

the unknown hands that toil to supply us with food and clothing;

the anonymous benefactors who transmit the wealth of their knowledge to us;

the conversation of a friend;

the shelter of our home;

the sweet responsibility of family;

the happiness of building for the future;

the renewal of our strength...

Many people are waiting for spectacular events of "worldly good-luck" in order to express their gratitude to heaven.

However, we Christians know that the blessings of Divine Providence enrich every aspect of our lives at every moment.

There is nothing meaningless on our pathway.

Every gift from the Heavenly Father is precious in the arena of our lives.

Therefore, utilizing the patrimony that the Lord has loaned us in our unceasing service of the Good, let us then learn to give thanks.

~ 156 ~

Relatives

If anyone does not provide for his own kin, and especially for his own family, he has denied the faith and is worse than an unbeliever. – Paul. (1 Tim. 5:8)

When it comes to ties of kinship, happenstance does not apply.

The subtle principles of the Law apply to blood ties.

Since we are compelled by causes from the past to come together in the present, it is crucial that we joyfully pay the debts that draw us to certain souls so that we may settle our debts to humanity.

It is futile to run from the creditors who live under the same roof with us, for time waits implacably for us, constraining us to liquidate every one of our debts.

There are those with sugar-sweet, edifying voices who preach salvation, but who are extremely intolerant in the home, bringing imbalanced energies to their daily chores.

Of course, the familial team in this world is not always a bed of roses. Quite often, it is a thorn bush of worries and anxieties requiring sacrifice. However, although we need to have a firm attitude in order to temper our affections, we can never cleanse the wounds of our home with the whip of violence or the plaster of negligence.

In keeping with the Apostle's warning, if we fail to care for our own family, we are denying our faith.

Relatives are works of love that the Merciful Father has given us to accomplish. Let us help them with cooperation and caring, attending to the designs of true fraternity. It is only by employing patience, understanding, tolerance and goodness on the narrow shores of the home that we will be able to serve victoriously on the sea of broad experiences.

~ 157 ~

Children

"See that you do not despise one of these little ones…" – Jesus. (Mt. 18:10)

When Jesus said not to despise little children, he was expecting from us not only providential measures having to do with bread and clothing.

It is not enough to feed starving little mouths or to cover cold little bodies. It is essential to provide them with moral shelter, which guarantees the reborn spirit the work environment needed for its sublimation.

Many parents guarantee their children material comfort, but relegate their soul to lamentable neglect.

Truancy in the streets produces delinquents who end up in prisons or mental hospitals, but spiritual laxity in the home creates social demons of perversity and madness, who, aided by money or social status, often spend much time spreading misery, suffering, darkness and ruin with deplorable impunity before earthly justice.

Therefore, do not despise children by handing them over to the impulses of the animalized nature.

Remember that all of us are being educated and re-educated before the Divine Master.

A plate of food is important for a person's growth, but we must not forget that "man does not live by bread alone."

Let us remember children's spiritual nourishment by means of our attitudes and examples, warnings and corrections at the right time, for to abandon them morally in their tasks of today will be to condemn them to self-contempt in the works they will be accountable for tomorrow.

~ 158 ~

Without Love

But whoever hates his brother is in darkness and walks in darkness, and does not know where he is going, because the darkness has blinded his eyes. – John. (1 Jn. 2:11)

If you do not know how to cultivate genuine fraternity, you will be fatally attacked by pessimism, just as dry land will undergo the accumulation of dust.

Everything bothers those who harbor intransigence.

Those who avoid the endeavors of love are profoundly sad due to the bitterness of the intolerance with which they nourish themselves.

When invited to participate in a team endeavor, they say that people are morally bankrupt.

When they attend a place of worship, they see evil and disillusion everywhere.

When called to act for charity, they see suffering brothers and sister as possible enemies and walk away in anger.

When invited to this or that celebration of happiness, they decline, disillusioned, seeing evil and mud in the smallest displays of festive beauty.

They live in the world amidst bitterness and suspicion.

No amount of caring is enough for them. They drain people's energy wherever they go with their weeping, complaining and lamenting...

They have no sure direction. They say that society and family have rejected them.

Incapable of loving their neighbor, they walk the earth under the heavy fog of selfishness that holds us in the narrow circle of our own wants without any expression of respect for other people's.

They say they are misunderstood, but it is because they do not wish to understand.

Without love, they dry up the machinery of life and lose their spiritual sight.

Inaccessible to the Good, they become representatives of evil.

If pessimism draws nigh to your spirit, shield yourself in prayer and ask the Lord to increase your resistance against the assault of the darkness.

Let us learn to live with everyone, tolerating so that we may be tolerated, helping so that we may be helped, and love will enable us to live, useful and optimistic, in the luminous atmosphere in which struggle and labor are blessings of hope.

~ 159 ~

With Love

Whoever loves his brother is in the light, and in him there is no offence. – John. (1 Jn. 2:10)

Those who love their neighbor know, above all, to understand. And those who understand know to free their eyes and ears from the poisonous enticement of offence in order to help, instead of accusing or disserving.

It is necessary to bring the heart to dwell in the light of true fraternity in order to realize that we are each other's brothers and sisters, children of just one Father.

As long as we keep ourselves in the dark phase of being attached solely to ourselves, we imprison ourselves in selfishness and expect others to love us. During this unfortunate time, we only know how to want for ourselves, using others as instruments of our own satisfaction.

But if we really do love the brother or sister on our path, the scenery of our life changes because the light of love bathes our vision.

Therefore, love, and just as mud can never offend the light, offence can never touch you.

You will know that misery is the fruit of ignorance, and thus you will help victims of wrongfulness, finding in them your own brothers and sisters in need of support and understanding.

You will learn to listen without disgust even if crime reaches your ears, and you will help your adversary even when you feel offended, because forgiveness combined with complete forgetfulness for the blows you have received will arise spontaneously in your spirit, just as tolerance is natural for the spring that receives the stones that are cast into it.

Love and you will understand.

Understand and you will serve more and more each day, for you will dwell within the glory of the light, inaccessible to any incursion of the darkness.

~ 160 ~

In the Everyday Struggle

For whatever a man may sow, that he also will reap. – Paul. (Gal. 6:7)

It is not necessary to die physically in order to grasp the law of compensation.

Let us observe the everyday struggle.

Those who are indifferent to the suffering of their neighbor will receive indifference from others regarding their own suffering.

If we isolate ourselves from social life, depressing loneliness will be the world's response to us.

If we are strict towards others, we will be judged with strictness and harshness by others.

If we practice hostility and aversion in society or in the family, we will experience antipathy and mistrust amongst neighbors and relatives.

If we insult our job with laziness, our job will relegate us to ineptitude.

A gesture of kindness towards an unknown person on the street will win us the fraternal concourse of anonymous groups around us.

Small sowings of goodness create blessed springs of happiness.

A job well done produces the treasure of competence.

Attitudes of understanding and kindness result in sympathy and respect.

Optimism and hope, stateliness of character and pure intentions attract invaluable opportunities of help on our behalf.

Every single day is a time of sowing.

Every single day is time of reaping.

One does not have to cross the darkness of the grave in order to come face to face with justice. In accordance with the principles of cause and effect, we are incessantly confronted with its guidance at every moment of our life.

~ 161 ~

In the Common Effort

Do you not know that a little yeast leavens the whole lump? – Paul. (1 Cor. 5:6)

Let us remember that our thoughts, words, attitudes and actions are mental molds for those who accompany us.

Each and every day we, in turn, experience other people's influence in the construction of our destiny.

And since we receive according to what we attract and reap according to what we have sown, it is essential that we give others the best of ourselves so that others may give us the best of themselves.

All your thoughts act upon the minds around you.

All your words generate impulses in those who hear you.

All your written sentences create images in those who read them.

All your actions are living models that influence those who surround you.

No matter how hard you try to isolate yourself, you will always be a living part in the machine of life.

The tires that roll on the ground guarantee the comfort and safety of the car.

We are a team of workers acting in a perfect interdependence.

The quality of our effort gives rise to the success or failure of the whole.

Our life, in whatever area of the struggle, is a grand, molding workshop.

We can either enslave ourselves to the captivity of the darkness, or free ourselves to the glory of the light, depending on the living molds that our guidelines and actions establish.

Let us remember correctness and uprightness in our most obscure gestures.

Let us remember the lesson of the Gospel.

"A little yeast leavens the whole lump."

Let us render our own pathway a blessed fountainhead of work and fraternity, assistance and hope so that our Industrious Today may become a Divine Tomorrow for us.

~ 162 ~

Within the Struggle

"I do not ask that you take them out of the world, but that you deliver them from evil." – Jesus. (Jn. 17:15)

Do not ask to be delivered from your suffering.

Pray for the strength to bear it with serenity and heroism so that you do not lose the advantages of experiencing it.

Do not ask for the stones to be removed from your pathway.

Insist on receiving thoughts that will help you take advantage of them.

Do not demand that your adversaries be driven away.

Ask for resources for your own elevation so that you may transform their sentiments.

Do not plead for the end of your problems.

Look for ways to overcome them and to assimilate their lessons.

Nothing exists without a reason.

The Wisdom of the Lord does not leave room for uselessness.

Suffering has its invaluable function in the plans of the soul, just as the storm has its important place in the economy of nature.

From the moment it sprouts, the tree grows and produces, overcoming all resistance.

The body of the creature develops amidst all kinds of dangers.

Let us accept our day of service wherever and however the Wise Will of the Lord has determined it.

In presenting the disciples to the Heavenly Father, the Master said: "I do not ask that you take them out of the world, but that you deliver them from evil."

The earth has its mission and its grandeur; let us deliver ourselves from the evil that operates within us and we will receive its divine help, becoming, along with it, living agents of the Blessed Kingdom of God.

~ 163 ~

Let Us Learn with Jesus

Forbearing and forgiving one another if there is any complaint. Just as Christ has forgiven you, so you should forgive one another. – Paul. (Col. 3:13)

Any activity by a group is impossible unless it is based on tolerance.

Let us learn with Christ.

People experience the law of cooperation in their own bodies; without such law, they would not be able to live on the earth.

If the stomach did not bear the excesses of the mouth; if the hands did not obey the impulses of the mind; and if the feet did not bear the weight of the organic machine, physical harmony would be impossible.

Complaining disfigures the dignity of work and keeps it from getting done.

It is crucial to renounce our petty desires so that we may acquire the capacity of sacrifice, which will serve as a structure for our sublimation at higher levels.

For our labor to elevate us, we must elevate it.

For our task to help us, we must make ourselves available to help it.

Let us remember that the supreme head of teams involving Christian service is always Jesus. As members of them, our chance to do something is, by itself, a valuable reward.

Therefore, let us forget all evil so that we may do all the goodness within our reach.

And so that we may act according to these rules, we must forbear with one another as brothers and sisters, learning with the Lord, who shows infinite tolerance towards us.

~ 164 ~

In God's Presence

"Our Father…" – Jesus. (Mt. 6:9)

For Jesus, the existence of God is no reason for quarrels and altercations.

He does not ask about the nature of the Eternal One.

He does not ask where he lives.

He does not see Him as being the obscure and impersonal cause of the universe.

He simply calls Him "our Father."

In moments of work and prayer, joy and suffering, he looks to the Supreme Lord in the position of a loving and trusting son.

The Master sets the standard for the attitude we should have in God's presence.

There is no pointless research.

There is no urgent questioning.

There is no inappropriate demanding.

There is no irreverent defining.

Whenever you pray, go into the secret chamber of your conscience and entrust yourself to God as our Heavenly Father.

Be sincere and faithful.

In our condition as needy children, let us give ourselves faithfully to Him.

Do not ask if God is a generating focal point of worlds or if He is a force that radiates life.

We do not yet have the intelligence capable of reflecting His grandeur, but we do have hearts that can sense His love.

Therefore, let us seek our Father above all else, and God, our Father, will hear us.

~ 165 ~

Do Not Doubt

He who doubts is like a wave on the sea, blown and tossed about by the wind. — James. (James 1:6)

In your acts of faith and hope, do not let doubt interpose itself like a shadow between your needs and the power of the Lord.

In your endeavors, the coagulating power of your thoughts proceeds from yourself, from deep within your soul, because only those who have faith can persevere in climbing the steps that will take them to heights they hope to reach.

On the outer plane, doubt may help with experimentation in this or that area of material progress; hesitation in our inner world, on the other hand, undoes our finest energies.

Those who doubt themselves disturb the divine help within them.

No one can help those who do not help themselves.

Understanding the imperative of trust that should guide our course ahead, let us insist on the Good and seek it with all the strength we have.

Let us abandon hurry and turn our backs on discouragement.

It does not matter if our conquest is triumphant today or tomorrow. What matters is working and doing the best we can, here and now, because life will bring us what we seek.

Pressing forward without hesitating; loving, learning and helping tirelessly – that is the formula for walking successfully to our victory. And on this tireless journey, let us not forget that doubt will always be like the cold of defeatism leading us towards denial and death.

~ 166 ~

Let Us Follow Him

"Whoever follows me will not walk in darkness." Jesus. (Jn. 8:12)

There are those who wonder at Christ's glory. But pure and simple wonder may turn into useless ecstasy.

There are those who believe in the Lord's promises. However, this belief by itself may generate fanaticism and strife.

There are those who defend Jesus' revelation. Nevertheless, defense, considered in isolation, may lead to sectarianism and blindness.

There are those who trust the Divine Master. However, stagnant trust may be an inert force.

There are those who wait for the Eternal Benefactor. Nevertheless, expectancy without work may be useless anxiety.

There are those who praise the Savior. Praise by itself, however, may become unproductive adoration.

The word of the Heavenly Messenger is clear and incisive: "Whoever follows me will not walk in darkness."

If you have love the Gospel, do not place yourself outside of Christian service.

Seek the Lord, following his footsteps.

That is the only way we will be with Christ, receiving his magnificent light.

… 167 …

Let Us Watch Ourselves

He who says that he remains in him must walk as he walked. – John. (1 Jn. 2:6)

There are those who say they live with the goodness of Jesus, but they do not hesitate to attack others with their slander and cruelty.

There are those who say they understand the Divine Master's optimism, but they do not waver at focusing on the darkness of pessimism and despair.

There are those who proclaim the fraternity of Christ, yet they encourage schism and discord.

There are those who exalt the incessant work of the Lord to spread the Good, but they are settled in the web of idleness and self-indulgence.

There are those who praise the humility of the Eternal Friend, yet they complicate all the issues of the way.

There are those who glorify the patience of the Sublime Instructor, but they hold to the boulder of aggressiveness and intolerance.

If we profess ourselves as learners of the Gospel, then let us watch our own steps.

Let us remember that the name of Jesus has been committed into our hands.

Grasping that fact, let us endear ourselves to the Divine Model.

When the apostle states, "He who says that he remains in him must walk as he walked" obviously means to say, "Those who claim to be Jesus' followers must imitate his behavior, seeking to live according to the Master's exemplary life."

~ 168 ~

Between the Cradle and the Grave

Not minding things that can be seen, but things that are unseen, for what can be seen is temporary, whereas what is unseen is eternal.
– Paul. (2 Cor. 4:18)

The flower we see soon wilts, but its fragrance, which escapes us, enriches the economy of the world.

The monument that impresses us will suffer the actions of time, but the invisible ideal that inspired it shines eternally in the artist's soul.

The Acropolis in Athens, admired by millions of eyes, has been wasting away little by little; nevertheless, the Greek culture that produced it is immortal in its earthly glory.

The cross that the people forced on Christ was an instrument of torture seen by everybody, but the Lord's spirit, which nobody sees, is a sun that has grown bigger and bigger with the passage of time.

Do not get too attached to transitory flesh.

Tomorrow, the infancy and youthfulness of the body will become middle- and old- aged.

The lands you possess today will inevitably be divided up in the future. The ornaments you are proud of today will turn into dust and ashes. The money that serves you today will pass into different hands.

Use what you see to accumulate what you do not yet see.

Between the cradle and the grave, human beings have the right to make use of the land in order to perfect themselves.

Therefore, do not get attached to the deceitful shell of beings and things. Learning and struggling, working and serving with humility and patience in constructing the Good, you will accumulate in your soul the richness of life eternal.

~ 169 ~

Let Us Seek Eternity

Although the outer man is wasting away, the inner man is being renewed day by day. – Paul. (2 Cor. 4:16)

Do not allow yourself to be discouraged when faced with changes in your physical equipment.

Let us seek Eternity.

Diseases do not touch the soul if they are not the result of regrets of the conscience.

Old age does not affect the spirit if we are trying to live according to the light of immortality.

Youthfulness is not a state of the flesh.

There are young people in the world who have hearts filled with dreadful ruins.

Let us remember that the inner man continues to be renewed. The struggle enriches it with experience; pain purifies its emotions and sacrifice tempers its character.

The incarnate spirit goes through constant transformations outwardly in order to purify itself and evolve inwardly.

Remember that the time you spend on earth is but a spiritual journey.

Just as a traveler wears sandals, wearing them out along the way, our soul makes use of forms, utilizing them on the ascending march towards the Great Light.

Therefore, open your heart's receiver to the sublime wave of the noblest ideals and the most beautiful thoughts. Let us learn to live far from the termite of discouragement, and our spirit, even if faced with the hardest trials of infirmity or old age, will be like a shining sun, expressing itself in songs of work and joy, expelling darkness and bitterness, wherever we may be.

~ 170 ~

Labeling

But whoever does not have the spirit of Christ is not of him. – Paul. (Rom. 8:9)

Labeling does not bring tranquility.

Let us delve into the essence.

There are praises in Christ's memory, written on banners that cause animosity amongst brothers and sisters.

There are symbols of Christ in many courts[3] that often exalt only injustice.

There are precious references to Christ, spoken in voices that are highly characteristic of the world's culture, voices which in the name of the Gospel only spread misery and ignorance.

There are oaths that swear on Christ, spoken in conversations that constitute long corridors towards the darkness.

---

[3] Many courts, banks and other public buildings in Brazil have a crucifix or some other Catholic symbol affixed to one of the walls. – Tr.

There are verbal invocations to Christ, done in purely commercial operations, but which are actually disguised attacks on the harmony of the conscience.

Let us meditate on the extent of our moral duties in the circle of responsibilities we have embraced with the Christian faith.

Jesus remains on images, posters, flags, medals and adornments, and in hymns, poems, narratives, lectures, sermons, studies and arguments, but this means very little if we do not possess his living lessons in our heart and mind.

It is always easy to express enthusiasm and conviction, and to make solemn promises and well-spoken sentences.

Let us be on guard, however, against the danger of labeling. As the Apostle says, let us not forget that if we do not have the spirit of Christ, then we are still a long ways from him.

~ 171 ~

Bearing Witness

To this you were called, because Christ suffered for you, leaving you an example that you should follow in his steps. – Peter. (1 Pet. 2:21)

Many people complain about the moral struggle in which they feel involved after having accepted the Gospel.

They feel they have changed; they are on a different course.

They are no longer immersed in the dark currents of vanity.

They no longer take pleasure in pride.

They no longer sympathize with self-centeredness.

They no longer involve themselves in disharmony.

Consequently, with souls unburdened by having lost their former chains of illusion, they find that their feelings are more acute, thereby increasing their afflictions in life.

They feel exposed to the dolorous process of purification, and they believe their own trials are harder than other people's. But in this spiritual sublimation to which they bear witness, other children of the earth come in contact with the Gospel, discovering the magnificence of the Christian life and spreading its divine light.

Therefore, if we feel that our inner life is in disarray when faced with problems caused by faith, let us bravely overcome life's conflicts, always choosing to deny ourselves on behalf of the general good, for we were not brought into communion with Jesus simply for the act of believing in him, but for our contribution to expanding the Kingdom of God at the cost of our own renewal.

Nobody should step back when faced with suffering. Let us learn to use it to construct a more effective life filled with peace and light, service and fraternity, cheerfulness and joy, for according to the Gospel, "to this we were called" by the example of the Divine Master, who denied himself on our behalf and left us the standard of the spiritual heights to which we must strive.

~ 172 ~

Before Christ, the Liberator

"I am the door." – Jesus. (Jn. 10:7)

According to the lexicon, the word "door" means "an opening in a wall on the ground floor, offering entrance and exit."

However, symbolically speaking, the world is replete with deceptive doors. They offer entrance but not exit.

Some of these doors are avidly fought over by men and women, who, in their desperation to acquire ephemeral possessions, are not cautious against the perils they represent.

Many of them knock at the door of wealth, but after being welcomed, they awake, imprisoned in the torments of greed.

Many others force open the door to the illusion of human power, only to find themselves gripped in the claws of suffering.

A huge number go through the door of earthly pleasures, but soon realize they are caught in the mesh of affliction and death.

And many others cross the threshold of the public spotlight, eager for popularity and influence, but end up cloistered in the dungeon of despair.

Christ, however, is the door to the Abundant Life.

With him, we submit ourselves to the will of the Heavenly Father, and according to that guideline, we accept life as a time of learning and service for our own growth towards immortality.

Consequently, be careful about which door you use in your daily struggle, for only by means of Christ's teachings will you set out on the pathway to true liberty.

~ 173 ~

Before the Light of the Truth

"You shall know the truth, and the truth will set you free" – Jesus. (Jn. 8:32)

The word of the Master is clear and secure.

We will not be set free by "aspects of the truth" or by the "temporary truths" we hold to in the circle of our impassioned affirmations.

In politics, philosophy, science and religion, many are attached to certain aspects of the truth and make their lives a desperate battlefield in order to defend it, whereas they are really just prisoners of their own point of view.

Many accept the truth, spread its teachings, advocate its cause, and proclaim its merits. However, the truth that sets us free is that which we come to know in our incessant activity for the Eternal Good.

To grasp the truth is to comprehend our responsibilities.

To discern the truth is to renew our own understanding and make our life a field of responsibility for what is *best*.

True freedom can be found only in our submission to a duty faithfully fulfilled.

Therefore, to know the truth is to realize the meaning of life.

And to realize the meaning of life is to grow in service and constant self-perfection.

Thus, examine your position before the Light...

Those who only glimpse the dazzling glory of this reality talk much but do little. On the other hand, those who grasp its indefinable grandeur do much and talk little.

~ 174 ~

Out-Stretched Hands

"Stretch out your hand." And he stretched it out and it was restored, whole like the other.
– (Mk. 3:5)

In every house of religious faith, there are believers with hands out-stretched, pleading for help...

Afflicted souls reveal anxiety, weakness, hopelessness and infirmities of the heart.

Are not all of us, incarnates and discarnates alike, who ask for something from Divine Providence, like the man with the withered hand?

Caught in the labyrinth we have created for ourselves, we pray for help from the Divine Master...

However, let us ponder our attitude.

It is all right to ask, and nobody can stop any manifestation of humility, repentance or intercession.

But it is crucial to examine the way it is received.

Many people wait for a *materialized response* from Jesus.

This one hopes for money; that one counts on sudden social status; that one over there expects immediate changes to circumstances on his or her earthly pathway…

But let us observe the way the Master helped the man with the withered hand.

Jesus tells him to stretch out his withered hand, but when the man does so, Jesus does not give him bags of gold or privileges. He heals him. Jesus gives him the opportunity to serve.

The healed hand is as empty as it was in the first place.

This is because Christ restored to the man the blessing of working, thus acquiring sacred achievements for himself. Jesus sends him back to the redemptive toil for the Good, in which he is supposed to enlighten and ennoble himself.

This is an impressive lesson for all churches of the Christian community.

When you stretch out your hands to the Lord, do not expect ease, wealth or privileges … Learn to receive his assistance, for Divine Love will restore your energies but it will not offer you an escape from achievements requiring your own effort.

~ 175 ~

Change

But they did not welcome him, because he was on his way to Jerusalem. – (Lk. 9:53)

This verse from Luke is worthy of comment.

When the Samaritans saw that Jesus and the disciples were going to Jerusalem, they refused to welcome them.

The Samaritans identified them by their look.

If they had been travelers on their way to somewhere else, perhaps they would have offered them accommodation, comfort, joy...

Does the same thing not apply even today with the true followers of the Master?

For us, Jerusalem in this verse symbolizes *bearing witness to the faith*.

And all it takes is for someone to walk resolutely on this path for ordinary people, directionless and argumentative, to shut the doors of their hearts to him or her.

Those who are careless, who are bent on easy pleasures, are immediately welcomed by the new Samaritans of the world.

On the earth, restless women and well-dressed, deceitful and spiritually sick men have a large number of friends for the time being.

However, when followers of Jesus wake up on the human pathway, realizing they have to bear witness to their trust in God by denying their old ways, then in most cases they must proceed all alone.

This is because on such occasions they show themselves to have been changed.

They do not display the normal impression of persons seeking self-satisfaction.

They are individuals who have resolved to renounce their defects and to eliminate them at the cost of enormous effort in order to espouse the redemptive cross that will identify them as belonging to the Divine Master…

For this reason, they will not be fully acknowledged even in their own homes, because they have undergone a profound metamorphosis… They now show signs of those who have taken the pathway of definitive inner renewal towards God, willing to devote themselves to the Eternal Good and to uplift their heart on the great pathway…

~ 176 ~

Need for the Good

And let us consider how we may spur one another on towards charity and good works.
– Paul. (Heb. 10:24)

Many institutions of the Christian life, revered for their programs and fundamentals, suffer incalculable harm due to the thoughtlessness with which many of their members watch each other.

Here, someone is commenting on the seedy past of a person who is trying to recover with dignity; there, small, unfortunate actions are being analyzed through the dark lens of sarcasm and criticism…

Indiscriminate criticism and disapproval, however, may spill over into this family of ideals, like corrosive rain on a newly-planted crop, destroying seeds and blooms, and poisoning a harvest bound for the barns of general progress.

One can never repeat too often the need for forgiveness, goodness and optimism in our chores and activities.

Let us remember that, with our help, everything today can be better than it was yesterday, and everything tomorrow will be better than it is today.

Evil, in any circumstance, means disharmony before the Law, and every instance of imbalance will rebound in difficulty and suffering.

Let us examine one another under the light of fraternity so that fraternity may light the pathway of our destinies.

Without persevering in the Good, there is no path to happiness.

This is why the Apostle Paul tells us: "And let us consider how we may spur one another on towards charity and good works," because only according to that guideline will we be serving to build the Kingdom of Love.

~ 177 ~

Wealth for Heaven

"Store up treasures in heaven..." –
Jesus. (Mt. 6:20)

Those who are improperly troubled at seeing the triumph and prosperity of many impious, self-centered people are actually showing envy, rebelliousness, ambition and discouragement. It is crucial not to be this way!

After all, who can say that he or she truly deserves to possess such earthly advantages?

If we see men and women lacking moral scruples possessing the transitory assets of the world, let us feel pity for them, instead.

The word of Christ is clear and irrefutable: "Store up treasures in heaven."

This means, "Let us accumulate inner assets in order to partake of glory eternal!"

The gallery of the carnal evidence will always be ephemeral.

Physical beauty, fleeting power, temporary property and amassed wealth may be a simple attribute of the human mask, which time tirelessly transforms.

Let us accumulate goodness and learning, understanding and sympathy.

Without the treasure of personal education, our entrance into heaven will be pointless, for we will be unable to attune ourselves to the appeals of the Higher Life.

Let us grow in virtue and incorporate true wisdom, for tomorrow you will be visited by the leveling hand of death, and you will possess only the noble or degrading qualities that you have accumulated within yourself.

178

Reverence and Compassion

Let us serve God joyfully, with reverence and compassion. – Paul. (Heb. 12:28)

"Let us serve God joyfully," says the apostle, but he does not forget to emphasize the way we should serve him.

We are not to spread sadness in our endeavors for the Good.

All the elements of nature obey the Laws of the Lord, revealing joy.

The constellation shines at night.

The sun pours forth its heat and light.

The earth is covered with flowers and greenery.

The spring has its peculiar tune.

The bird sings its songs of praise.

Therefore, it would not be right to bring pessimism and bitterness to the service the Master has prepared for us.

The contentment of helping is one of the signs of our faith.

Nevertheless, our joy must not be excessive.

Neither inappropriate noise-making, nor improper concepts.

Neither unworthy speech, nor boisterous laughter that may suggest sarcasm and disdain.

Let us serve joyfully, with reverence and compassion.

Reverence towards the Lord; compassion towards our neighbor.

You cannot personalize the All-Merciful in order to please him, but we can serve him daily in the person of our brothers and sisters in the daily struggle.

Thus, let us drive the car of our service on the road of respect and charity, and we will find the joy that can never be extinguished.

~ 179 ~

Let Us Watch Our Hands

...he showed them his hands... - (Jn. 20:20)

When he reappeared to the disciples after his death, Jesus identified himself and let them see his injured body, especially his hands...

The hands that had restored sight to the blind, lifted up paralytics, healed the sick, and blessed the elderly and children, now bore the marks of sacrifice.

Injured by the nails of the cross, they brought to mind his supreme selflessness.

The hands of the Divine Worker did not receive from the world only the calluses of hard work at the plow of the Good; they also received bloody and dolorous wounds...

This lesson reminds us of the activity of hands in every corner of the globe.

The heart inspires.

The brain thinks.

The hands accomplish.

Everywhere, human life is carried on due to hands that command and obey.

Hands that guide; that construct; that sow; that caress; that help; that teach ... And hands that kill; that injure; that stone; that beat; that burn; that curse...

Our hands are living antennae that exteriorize our spiritual life.

Therefore, think carefully about what you do each day.

Do not forget that, after death, our hands show the marks of our passage on the earth. Those of Christ, the Eternal Benefactor, showed the wounds received from the divine harvest of love. Yours, tomorrow, will also speak of you in the spirit world, where, with the earthly experience ended, each person will reap life's blessings or lessons according to his or her works.

~ 180 ~

Christmas

"Glory to God in the Highest, and on earth peace to men of goodwill." – (Lk. 2:14)

Announcing the Great Renewer, the angelic legion at the manger spoke no word of violence.

Glory to God in the Divine Universe.

Peace on earth.

Goodwill to men and women.

Bequeathing the new age of safety and tranquility to the world, the Supreme Father did not vest the Heavenly Ambassador with powers to injure or destroy.

No punishment for the greedy rich.

No punishment for the desperate poor.

No disdain for the weak.

No condemnation for sinners.

No hostility toward the proud Pharisee.

No anathema against the unaware gentile.

Using the hands of Jesus, the Divine Treasure was poured out for the work of goodwill.

The justice of "an eye for an eye and a tooth for a tooth" had finally encountered Love ready and willing for sublime selflessness all the way to the cross.

Amazed before the light born in the stable, people and animals expressed indescribable joy.

From that unforgettable moment on, the earth would be renewed.

The torturer would be worthy of compassion.

The enemy would become a misguided brother or sister.

The criminal would be regarded as ill.

In Rome, the people would gradually cease the slaughter in the circus. In Sidon, slaves would no longer have their eyes gouged out by the cruelty of their masters. In Jerusalem, the sick would no longer be relegated to the valleys of filth.

Jesus brought the message of true fraternity, and, revealing it, he passed victoriously from the straw manger to the bloody cross.

Brothers and sisters: you, who hear the sweet echoes of the angels' miraculous song at Christmas, remember that the Master came to us so that we may love one another.

Christmas! Good News! Goodwill!

Let us extend sympathy to all, and let us truly begin to live with Jesus in the splendor of a new day.

Made in the USA
Charleston, SC
25 October 2013